T0197130

A New Beautiful: Overcoming Life's Obstacles

Ordinary Women, Sharing Extraordinary Stories

JENNIFER PULLARA

authorHOUSE®

AuthorHouse™
1663 Liberty Drive
Bloomington, IN 47403
www.authorhouse.com
Phone: 1 (800) 839-8640

Published by AuthorHouse 08/19/2015

ISBN: 978-1-5049-2357-6 (sc)
ISBN: 978-1-5049-2356-9 (e)

Library of Congress Control Number: 2015911398

Print information available on the last page.

I dedicate this book to my two, amazing children.

From the moment I held each of them in my arms,
I knew that I wanted them to be forever surrounded
by beautiful people, and in turn grow-up to be
independent, confident adults, with kind, gentle hearts.

May you always have beautiful souls and view
the world through a *beautiful lens*, just as the
inspirational women in this book have shown me
through acts of courage, love, and perseverance.

CONTENTS

INTRODUCTION

Life has a beautiful way of teaching lessons through the challenges you face. The ways in which your mind approaches the challenge, the emotional stance you take, and the people that support you, all play a role in the way you overcome those obstacles.

Now, in the year 2015, social media has a way of presenting *beautiful* with glam, glitter, and fashion. Advertisements have a focus around skinny women, outrageous successes in acting and highlight song and dance. There are places for these talents in our world, but in this book I want to focus the reader's attention on everyday women that had everyday problems and to no fault other than *fate* they had to make choices. As you read their stories you will be astonished at the strength they found within themselves to overcome personal challenges and redefine the beauty that lies within their hearts, minds, and souls.

Each chapter is written by a different woman. The unique aspect of this book is how the voice of the woman shines through. If you listen carefully as you read, you will not only hear a story, but will feel strength and determination. You may even be quite inspired. The authors of these stories are just ordinary woman, but with extraordinary compassion, sensitivity, and drive. Their understanding of what *life* is has guided them through difficult life events.

Challenges are part of life and can redefine who you are. This type of *beautiful*, doesn't just happen by accident, but rather by very purposeful thought, genuine love, and mental strength. These *beautiful* women battled through physical, emotional, and mental suffering, struggle, tragedy, illness, and hardship but it all led them to redefine themselves and become a ***New Beautiful***.

The amazing women who contributed to this book are:

Dr. Jacqueline Agresta

Dr. Ceil Candreva

Ms. Kristen Cacioppo

Mrs. Anne-Marie Dunn

Anonymous

Mrs. Nicole Fatscher

Ms. Tammy Kilkenny

Mrs. Katherine McCullagh

Mrs. Laura Oweis

Dr. Jennifer Pullara

Mrs. Maria Saraceni

Mrs. Barbara Soldan

Ms. Krysten Soldan

Mrs. Laura Soldan

Mrs. Jeanne Squillante

Dr. Kathryn Struthers Ahmed

Dr. Wafa Deeb Westervelt

"As I write this I realize I have been through many different situations in my life which I have had to overcome. As I talk to other women I realize that I am not alone. I am not the only one with issues or hard times. The words we share with each other make us stronger and help us know we are not alone. No woman in this world is alone. There is always someone else who has been there. It may not be in the same way, but similar. It is up to us to reach out and help each other. In the moments I have felt weak, discouraged, and depressed I have gotten through because of the people around me. I have become a stronger woman because of my life experiences, but I didn't get through them alone. I am strong and I have succeeded. I am continually becoming *a New Beautiful*."

Please note: All the authors may have chosen to use pseudonyms for the names and places that appear in this book.

LIFE CHAPTERS

When someone dies there is a *cause of death*. But the real challenge in life is identifying the *cause of life.* How do you learn how to live?

Life is constructed of chapters, never knowing how long an episode will last makes planning for the future nearly impossible. Life, when left alone, takes care of itself. Nature is complex, yet so beautiful. Human influence brings chaos to nature. But whom do we choose to be? A part of nature or a human with free will to choose? Are things ever totally in our control? Or are they ever totally out of our control?

I think the purpose of life is to be happy. But the question is: *How do I create happiness?* Happiness is love, a joyful spirit… which lies within one's heart and soul. But only I can create happiness for myself. If I know this then why does a part of my heart feel cold and sad? What do I have to do to awaken my inner spirit? Or does that spirit lie in the past and it is time for a new spirit, a new chapter in my life to begin? When I choose a new plan, when I embrace my emotions, when I conquer a tribulation…a *New Beautiful* chapter begins…happiness returns.

TRUSTING MY JOURNEY

My husband, Pete and I returned from a doctor's visit to find my brother in my back garden crying. My brother is not the crying type. Besides the crying, my brother has this very distinct look on his face when he is upset and it is seared into my memory. I've only seen it two other times in my life. The first was in third grade when we witnessed a classmate get fatally hit by a car. The second was the day my father's doctor told us that his lung cancer was no longer treatable. The third time was now. I want to erase the news and make it all better. I need him to know that I will be okay.

Rolling into the restroom with my IV pole, I am the center of attention at chemotherapy. I am a freak of nature - One breast, no hair and eight months pregnant for the first time. I hate the looks of pity. In my estimation the worst part of having breast cancer is the attention. The looks of sympathy, the whispering behind your back, the glances down toward your breasts wondering if you've had reconstruction. It's really depressing and I just want it to

3

go away. So many questions about life within me – life without me.

As a social worker my job is to help others. I don't like attention or focus on me. I would always prefer to hear about another person and their life rather than to talk about me. I work in an elementary school and as far as I'm concerned, I have the best job in the universe. I get to help children and families with issues that might interfere with learning. When I was first diagnosed one of my earliest fears was how I would continue to work. At the time, I worked in a very close knit elementary school. My fear was that as soon as the staff knew I was sick they would never come to me asking for help for their students. I would sit in an empty quiet office waiting for students just thinking about cancer. For me, maintaining normalcy was paramount and I decided that I needed to keep my cancer a secret. I would tell a few select trustworthy friends but maintain privacy about my health from the rest of the staff and school families.

In early September, after my diagnosis, surgery and two months of chemo, I returned to school. I was six months pregnant. Most of the staff did not know I was pregnant when I left in June so the focus upon my return would be my big belly and my joyous news. Maybe no one would notice my wig, pale face, dark circles and lack of energy. Most of those symptoms could easily be attributed to pregnancy, right? All I had to do was get to December. Then I would go out on maternity and no one at work would ever know. As I left for work that first day back I stopped for a quick visit to the bathroom to be sick. This was not due to pregnancy or chemo. I was a nervous wreck about the wig on my head.

I told exactly four people at work. All were good friends who were supportive and loving with not an ounce of pity. They supported me and kept my secret. They protected me and made sure they kept my cover.

September to December was a blur. I was busy working, maintaining my cover and slipping out side doors to get to chemo in the city on time. The chemo was not as bad as Lifetime T.V. predicted it to be. I was not sick but I did suffer from insane constipation, numb fingers, fatigue, dehydration, black fingernails, anemia and short intense spans of grief which would dissipate as quickly as they came on. Oh and not to forget the heart palpitations that my husband could hear across the room. While most people gasp when they hear of a pregnant person with cancer I have to say being pregnant made it easier in a lot of ways. I had focus and purpose. I had to get better so I could care for this baby. I would push selfish thoughts about myself from my mind and instead focus on this baby that would need my attention and love.

Toward the end of my pregnancy I found out that someone had heard about my illness and told my principal and staff. At first I was angry but now I realize that the person who told must have had a greater need for attention and gossip than my need to maintain privacy.

Scarlett Jean arrived on December 30th 2003. A picture perfect doll with a perfectly rounded rosy face. Every specialist confirmed she was perfectly healthy with no impact from the chemo. The final scar left from an uphill battle. A good scar, a great scar. My Scarlett.

A year after my ordeal I was ready to move on. I had hair again. And when the scars were covered by clothing, the reconstruction looked pretty decent. I had every intention of having more children but chemo had really messed with my cycle and overall health. After a fertility doctor told me that I was in full blown menopause past the point of no return, I left his office in tears. I had to have more children. I couldn't imagine life for Scarlett without siblings. A big family was important to my husband and me. My brother was my closest friend growing up and my husband has nine siblings.

After a lot of late nights on the Internet looking up "fertility after cancer" and adoption websites, I had a plan. I had found a book that talked about all natural methods of ensuring health and getting pregnant.

My husband giggled when I told him my plans: acupuncture, herbs, a trip to Texas (to have a consult with the author), meditation and a major diet change. No processed foods. No white sugar. No alcohol. No dairy. I would eat fruits, vegetables, unprocessed whole grains and lean all natural meats and fish. He laughed because he knows me. Because I was always naturally thin, I ate whatever I wanted in my twenties. Chocolate donuts for breakfast with a glass of whole milk, a bacon cheeseburger with a side of fries for lunch and a rich dinner complete with cream sauces, gravy, pasta and of course I never missed dessert. I'm not sure if I ate any vegetables at all during my twenties. This "gift" of being thin also led me to believe that I was healthy. A cruel trick – just because you look healthy does not mean you are healthy. "One year," I told him. I would give it one year. What's one year of giving up my favorite foods? My backup plan was adoption. I would start the ball rolling for adoption and see which happened first. After a year I would have a baby or adopt one.

As with every plan and/or crisis in my life my husband, Pete was there supporting me and cheering me on. It isn't every man in the world who could make you believe you are beautiful even with a bald head, scars on a good portion of your body and reconstructed breasts…but my husband somehow did. I am a lucky woman.

Five years before being diagnosed with cancer I started in a doctoral program in Social Welfare. My dissertation, like all dissertations was a tremendous amount of stress. Anyone who has completed the daunting task of writing a dissertation knows that it is ping pong match between you and your academic advisor. You write a draft, pass to them and they hand it back with notes and revisions. This dance continues for years and this is after completing a pretty intense and thorough load of course work. It is a process over which a student has very little control. It involves a lot of waiting for professors to get back to you. My plan was to hand back drafts and revisions so that I would not have work hanging over my head. I could take charge and speed up the lofty process. It was my way to try to take control of a difficult task and help it to be over quickly. My advisor would often complain that I had the draft returned so quickly for her to read and revise again.

I mention this dissertation and my diet together for a reason. Everyone asks you "Is it genetic? – Do you have any family history of breast cancer?" It's human nature to look for cause and effect. I don't know why I got cancer, but I truly believe it was the combination of stress and poor diet. Toxins enter everyone's body all the time. My body was not able to deal with the toxin of stress because I gave it no ability to fight. I did not feed it the nutrients it needed to fight the battle. I also had no emotional ability to fight it. I had no relaxation techniques. My acupuncturist once told me not to flatter myself thinking I had so much more stress in my life than other people. She reminded me that I had no ability to cope with the stress. It is your job to give your body the physical and emotional tools to deal with stress.

So while I completely learned a new way to live, I worked on my packet for the adoption agency. I collected letters from loving friends, had a home study done by a social worker, and started to write our family profile for prospective birth mothers to choose from. This task along with my new diet, acupuncture, meditation and one year-old Scarlett kept me pretty busy.

Meditation was the most difficult prescription the doctor gave. I adjusted to my new diet and the headaches I suffered from my white sugar addiction faded. I felt great. My head was clear and my body felt like it was working so energetically. But stopping to meditate during my new mother days was difficult. When Scarlett napped I forced myself to go in my room, shut the door and spend 25 minutes alone with peaceful thoughts. After weeks of struggling to push out the mental list filled with laundry, food shopping, house projects and really focusing on giving my mind and body a complete break, I was finally able to meditate and relax.

About a month after this new regimen I noticed that every ounce of baby fat was gone and I was amazed at how lean I was. I was the thinnest I had been since college. This was unexpected but gave me the feeling that I had some sort of proof that I was making a change. Two months after that I was no longer in menopause and two months after that I dropped to the bathroom floor in tears of gratitude upon seeing the positive pregnancy test. Since then I have had three healthy babies.

It is politically incorrect to talk about God these days. People think you are a Holy roller, a weirdo, against science, or a follower of silly rules. I don't care. I prayed on my knees for God's grace begging for more children and continued good health. I never stopped asking. While I was pregnant and going through the chemotherapy I would ask God to protect my baby and would picture a shell like substance around my baby. I would visualize how God was keeping this baby safe from the drugs only allowing healthy nutrients and love to slip into the womb. I knew that God was keeping this baby safe for me. While trying to conceive after the chemotherapy, I knew that my prayers would be answered even if they were adjusted to God's plan for me and my journey to come.

After a very long road, I have learned to focus on the positive, take care of my physical and mental health, enjoy the moment, be thankful and to trust my journey.

And so I became a *New Beautiful.*

Religion Divides, Love Unites

In December 2012, my boyfriend and I went to visit his parents. While many couples in their late twenties spend time with each other's parents, this was no ordinary visit. For one, we were traveling to Dubai, an almost daylong journey from the West Coast of the United States, where I was living at the time. Secondly, this was the trip where Faisal was going to tell his parents that we were dating seriously and planning to get married. Although a visit such as this might likely be filled with joy and celebration, ours was one of anxiety and trepidation. While in much of the Western world it is a "tradition" in heterosexual relationships that the man "asks" the woman's parents for their "permission" to marry their daughter, in our case, we had to beg for his parents' approval of our impending cross-cultural, cross-religious union. This trip was the longest and most emotionally tumultuous eight days of my life.

Faisal grew up in a traditional Muslim household in India. His parents – and his extended family – are deeply religious people who pray the requisite five times each day and endeavor to live their lives piously. In India, in both Hindu and Muslim households, parents arrange most marriages. Nowadays, the prospective bride and groom do not meet at the altar, but rather their parents set them up and they date for a few months before getting married. In Faisal's family, many of the couples (including his parents) had arranged marriages, as is customary. A few of his older cousins had "love marriages" – as this type of non-arranged union is called – but they had all chosen their spouses from within their Indian Muslim community. Faisal's sister wanted to marry an Indian Muslim man she met while in college in the U.S., but he was part of a different sect of Islam than Faisal's family, and he had a traditional Hindu name (as his mother was raised Hindu but converted to Islam when she married his father). In order for this wedding to be acceptable, he had to convert to Faisal's family's sect of Islam, and the family wanted him to change his name to a traditionally Muslim name. While he did not change his name, this marriage – which did take place – was considered scandalous in Faisal's family, for his sister had married outside of their community. To Faisal's family, marriage and religion are not just personal decisions and preferences, but sharing a religion is an important aspect of being part of the Muslim community, particularly as Muslims are a marginalized minority in India. Marrying someone from within the community is not only a matter of religious beliefs, but also a matter of cultural practices. In short, I came as a complete shock to Faisal's family.

I grew up in the Midwestern U.S. in a nominally Protestant household. My sisters and I were baptized and confirmed, and we attended a private Episcopalian school. While we celebrated Christmas and Easter growing up, my family was not religious. My Episcopalian school was very liberal, and our weekly chapel services often incorporated traditions from many faiths, such as Judaism, the Bahá'í Faith, and traditional Native American religions. I was taught to be open and accepting of others, especially those who were different than me. This was not necessarily grounded in the Christian principles of love and acceptance but more so in an ethical conviction to treat others how I wanted to be treated and to respect people's individual and cultural differences. In my extended family, as is typical of many mainline Protestant Americans, everyone had "love marriages," and while most of my family members got married in a church and had a religious service, most of them are not particularly religious. Incidentally, my oldest sister had become very religious at the end of high school and ended up marrying a fellow Fundamentalist/Evangelical Christian from the South. My middle sister had fallen in love with her high school sweetheart, who happened to be a Catholic man from a small town in southern Germany. My parents and extended family accepted both of my sisters' husbands openly, only caring that my sisters were happy, not that these men's religious views differed from their own. To them, marriage is an individual decision, and it is not within the parents' purview to intercede in that decision. How two people work together to shape their marriage and family life is up to the individual couple and is less dictated by community norms.

From India and the Midwest, Faisal and I met as freshmen in college in Boston. We lived on the same floor and happened to meet each other on the first day of freshmen orientation – which was Faisal's third day in the U.S. From this initial meeting, a strong friendship developed, which morphed into a casual dating relationship towards the end of college. After college, we both worked in Boston, and while we had broken up, we remained extremely close friends, talking daily and seeing each other often. There was no denying that we had a strong connection and a unique friendship, but we both dated other people and frankly did not think too much about our relationship during these first few years out of college. Circumstances changed when, five years after college graduation, Faisal and I both happened to leave Boston on the same day. I was headed to graduate school on the West Coast, and Faisal would spend a year abroad in Dubai before returning to the U.S. for business school in Atlanta. Although we were geographically far apart, we remained emotionally close, continuing to speak on the phone multiple times each day, including as soon as I woke up each morning and as I was falling asleep each night. After about nine months, we realized we missed each other more than close friends might miss each other, and we decided we wanted to be together. Given our long history, our relationship – though it was long distance – was serious from the beginning. A year and a half later, we were en route to Dubai.

"As-Salaam-Alaikum," Faisal's dad happily greeted us when we arrived at the Dubai airport. "Wa-Alaikum-Salaam," I replied sheepishly as he shook my hand. My stomach was in knots as we drove back to their house, as Faisal had warned me that this might be a tense week. I had met his parents several times before; I had even visited their home in Houston when they lived there and had flown to India to attend his sister's wedding a few years earlier. They are generous and loving people who always welcomed me warmly. However, during those prior visits, I was always a "friend." I was never a girlfriend, and I was certainly not considered marriage material. We arrived in Dubai late in the evening, so we ate dinner as soon as we reached Faisal's parents' house and then retired to bed (in separate rooms) to rest after our long journey. I don't remember much about that dinner, except that the food was delicious – I love Indian food – and that his parents were just as warm and welcoming to me as they had been when I visited them previously. I didn't say much, partly because I was tired, partly because I was nervous and uncomfortable, and partly because much of the conversation took place in Urdu, a language I do not speak. The next morning Faisal's sister and her husband arrived; they had decided to join our trip to help ease potential tensions between Faisal's parents and us. I was exceedingly grateful that they were there, as they provided a kind of buffer that helped ameliorate some of the awkwardness I was feeling.

The first few days of our trip occurred in much the same manner as our initial dinner. I was very quiet, and everyone was very nice – though obviously there was a huge elephant in the room about Faisal and my relationship. Faisal engaged in many conversations with his parents during these days, in which I did not participate (primarily due to my own nerves and discomfort, not because they did not want me to participate). He spoke with each of his parents individually as well as with them together, and then he provided me with updates after these conversations occurred. Although these conversations were many and lengthy, the bottom line was that his parents were not accepting of our future marriage – unless I converted to Islam. If I did not convert, they would have to disown us. They would not be able to attend our wedding and would not associate with us afterwards. They felt that it was against their religion – and their worldview – for someone to marry outside of Islam, and they could not acknowledge or support such a union. Faisal knew that this would be their position, and though he had forewarned me, I was still shocked, confused, and devastated. How could parents disown their child for marrying someone he loved? From my socially and culturally constructed worldview, this simply made no sense and was not something I understood. From Faisal's parents' perspective, it was unfathomable that their son might marry someone who was not Muslim – someone whom he would not even ask to convert to Islam. As his mother said to his sister, "How could he even *think* of marrying her?" In their minds, it made no sense to marry someone who came from such a different religious background; it was simply not practical, let alone culturally acceptable.

As for converting to Islam, I simply was not comfortable doing so. It did not feel right to lie and say I believed something when in fact I did not. Although one potential argument was, "Well, if it doesn't actually mean anything to you, what's the harm in saying it?" (All you have to do to convert to Islam is repeat after an imam, "There is no true god but Allah, and Mohammed is His Prophet.) However, this felt disingenuous and disrespectful to Faisal's parents and the religion they hold sacred. I also half-heartedly suggested to Faisal that we just tell his parents I converted even though I wouldn't; this would eliminate the conflict, and they would never know the difference. Yet, Faisal did not feel comfortable lying to his parents about an issue that was of such importance to them. Faisal's parents were upset that Faisal would not ask me to convert – though of course it would have made his life much easier if I did. From Faisal's perspective, the difference in religion did not matter (he obviously is not as religious as his parents), and he also did not feel comfortable asking me to do something that he would not be willing to do himself (convert to a different religion).

About midway through our trip, we were all sitting in the living room. Faisal had told me that his parents wanted to speak to me about this issue, to hear what I had to say. It would be an understatement to say that I hate conflict and avoid it at all costs, so needless to say I was incredibly nervous about this impending conversation. But I knew it was coming and that I had to participate. Although that night is a bit of a blur, Faisal's dad began the dreaded family conversation by saying something to the effect of, "So, Kaitlyn, as you know, we've been talking to Faisal a lot this week, but now we'd like to hear from you." In response, I immediately burst into tears. Faisal's dad looked horrified, and his mom came over to me, gave me a hug, and started crying herself. I was so embarrassed. He hadn't even asked a question, and I hadn't said a word! I composed myself and insisted I was okay. Faisal's sister said, "Daddy, she's just like me – if anything is uncomfortable, she just cries." I felt like I was not putting my best foot forward, to say the least. Faisal's parents went on to explain how in their view, it was important – especially for the sake of future children – that the parents are of the same religion. They reiterated that they would like me to convert to Islam.

I explained – still rather choked up – that I felt uncomfortable converting, because it would be a lie; I would be saying I believed something that I did not actually believe. I said I would be more than willing to learn about Islam and to participate in various religious practices, such as fasting during Ramadan. I also said that I was willing to raise our children Muslim. When they said that would be difficult if I were not Muslim myself, I gave the example of my middle sister, who is raising her children Catholic, as that was important to her husband, though she did not convert to Catholicism. I told them that her husband takes the lead on the religious teachings in the house – he takes the older kids to church while my sister stays home with the baby – and when the kids ask my sister a religious question, she gives them the "Catholic" answer. At that time, their oldest child was ten years old, and this arrangement seemed to be working well for them. I proposed that Faisal and I would do something similar. When Faisal's mother said that the Quran states that a Muslim must marry another Muslim, Faisal's sister retorted that in fact, the Quran says that a Muslim must marry another "believer," but that if I "converted," I would not actually be a believer. She and her husband used their situation as an example, saying that while Faisal's brother-in-law was technically raised in a Muslim household, he is not religious at all; in fact, he is an atheist. When he "converted" to Faisal's family's sect of Islam, he did so in name only, not because he actually believed in what he was saying. In his mind, that was the easiest way for him to marry Faisal's sister – and at this point, he had solidified his place in the family as a good husband to Faisal's sister, so he could say these things. But, again, that scenario did not feel right for me. Although Faisal's dad kept saying that he was "sure" we would find a solution that was acceptable to all of us, we seemed to be at a standstill.

We remained at this standstill for a few more days, as Faisal kept rehashing the issue with his parents. His parents struggled to reconcile their love for their son with their faith in Islam and their commitment to their community. While they searched in vain for an answer, it eluded them. Either I converted to Islam, or they would have to disown us, as heartbreaking as that would be. Faisal, of course, was hoping that by this point in the trip, his parents would have moved away from their position and come to accept us, albeit perhaps reluctantly. He said to me, "Honestly, I thought that when they spent time with you they would just fall in love with you like I did and not worry about religion." Unfortunately, that is not what happened. I was too nervous and uncomfortable to be myself; I barely spoke throughout the trip. I felt I had let Faisal down. And he had done nothing but support me, comfort me and stand up for us. Ultimately, he told his mother, "I'm sorry that you feel this way, and we really want you to be a part of our lives. But I'm going to marry Kaitlyn." This was far and away the most selfless, romantic, and loving gesture anyone has ever done for me. I felt undeserving of such a principled and devoted man – someone who was willing to give up his parents (and most likely his entire extended family) for me. Was I worthy of such a thing? I couldn't be. How could I be responsible for my husband never speaking to his parents again? My stomach was in knots – again. I thought maybe I should just "convert" to Islam just to smooth over this rift I had caused between Faisal and his parents. Faisal reassured me that everything would be okay, that our life was "you and me," facing the world together as a team. We joked about what drama our future children might put us through one day. Although before our visit to Dubai I had no doubts about my love for Faisal and our future together, this trip solidified our bond and made me realize – on a completely new level – how much we loved and cared for each other. Despite feeling anxious, uncomfortable, and guilty throughout the entire trip, I also felt like the most fortunate person in the world. I had found the perfect partner for me.

Faisal's sister and brother-in-law left a day and a half before we did. We had one more, full day in Dubai and then were scheduled to leave the following morning at 5am. When the two of them left, they said they were sorry the issue hadn't been resolved and that the circumstances remained so grim. Faisal emailed his best friend and said the trip had been a "disaster"; I emailed my sister and said it had been "pointless." The next day – our last full day there – proceeded much as the others had, with many awkward silences and a lot of tension in the air. In the early afternoon, Faisal and I each went upstairs to take a nap. When we woke up, his mother was in the living room, and his father was upstairs resting. Faisal and his mom started to have a conversation in Urdu, so I had no idea what they were discussing, though the tone sounded upbeat. Seemingly out of nowhere, Faisal started talking – in English – about how in the U.S., many women wear strapless wedding dresses, to which his mom shook her head in disapproval. He also said that at American weddings, champagne toasts are part of the culture of celebration, to which she nodded in understanding. (In Islam, baring your shoulders is frowned upon and drinking alcohol is forbidden.) I was so confused – why was Faisal talking about these small wedding details, when his parents were never going to speak to us again?

From across the room, I gave him a look to convey this sentiment, to which he responded with a look that said, "Just trust me." He told me to go upstairs and bring down a wedding planning magazine that my sister had given me for Christmas. He showed it to his mom and turned to the page that showed different dress styles – sweetheart neckline, spaghetti straps, capped sleeves, etc. I had no idea why he was doing this; I was so confused. But I went along with it. Faisal's mom kept saying, "Well, we'll wait until Daddy wakes up," presumably to run something by him – but what, I did not know.

When Faisal's dad woke up from his nap, there was some conversing amongst the three of them in Urdu. I had no idea what was going on. Faisal's parents then explained that while we were all sleeping, Faisal's mom had conducted a Google search posing the question, "Can a Muslim man marry a Christian woman?" which led her to Bilal Philips' YouTube video titled, "Marriage to Non-Muslims: Contemporary Issues." Bilal Philips is a known imam and Islamic scholar who used to lead services at the mosque

Faisal's parents attended in Dubai. Faisal whispered that I was not going to like parts of this video, but to not object to the rationale presented. In this video Bilal Philips stated, "A Muslim male is allowed to marry two categories of non-Muslim females: either a Christian or a Jew... because of the fact that there still remains - in the books in which they believe - elements of revelation." He went to say that the husband is also not allowed to interfere with the wife's faith; she can – and should – worship as she chooses. (The rationale I did not like had to do with the reasoning behind why it was okay for a Muslim man to marry a Jewish or a Christian woman while it was not acceptable for a Muslim woman to marry a Jewish or a Christian man. But that was beside the point at this particular moment.)

We were all surprised, relieved, and happy to watch this video. I almost couldn't believe it! Were Faisal's parents changing their minds? Had they found a way to reconcile their faith with their love for their son? Thank you, Bilal Philips! While his parents respected Bilal Philips, Faisal's dad double-checked his interpretation of this issue with two other Islamic scholars whom he trusted. To our delight, these scholars agreed with this interpretation – a Muslim man could indeed marry a Christian woman! (We conveniently left out the fact that I don't actually identify as a practicing Christian.)

All of a sudden, the mood in the house changed drastically. Whereas a few hours earlier I believed Faisal's parents would never speak to us again, now everyone was talking excitedly about our upcoming wedding. Faisal's dad explained to me, "In our culture, when two people decide to get married, we believe they should get married as soon as possible. So, when we come to Atlanta for Faisal's graduation in May, you'll have the *nikah* [the Islamic marriage ceremony], and then we'd like to have a celebration in India in December. You can do whatever you'd like in the U.S. in between those times." I'm pretty sure I just nodded and whispered, "Okay." I was in shock. I still could not believe this was happening. As far as Faisal's parents were concerned, we were now officially engaged. Faisal explained the American custom of a man proposing with an engagement ring, to which his mom replied, "So give her one of my rings. Get engaged right now." Although I then tried on a few of her rings, her fingers are much smaller than mine, so this did not happen. Faisal explained that he wanted to pick out the ring himself and do a "proper" proposal (which he did a few months later). When we left, Faisal's parents told us they loved us and called me their daughter. We were married – both in a *nikah* ceremony and in a secular Western ceremony, in Boston the following November. We had additional celebrations in India exactly one year after our fated trip to Dubai.

Looking back, I remember how anxious and uncomfortable I felt – and then how relieved and overjoyed I was – during this trip. I feel so fortunate that Faisal's parents found this "loophole" that made all of us feel at peace with our decisions. I also learned how, despite my liberal upbringing, there will be cultural differences that I simply don't understand and that can't necessarily be "overcome" easily. Yet, just because I cannot fully understand other people's worldviews – because our lives, backgrounds, and experiences are uniquely our own – I can love them, and I can learn from them, and I can compromise with them. I admire Faisal's parents' faith greatly, and I admire the love they have for their son, who of course they would have been devastated to disown. Through this experience – and the continued navigation of Faisal and my cultural differences – I have grown as a person and developed into someone who honors others' perspectives in a new way. Through this experience, I have become a *New Beautiful.*

My Doctor's My Friend.
I'm Not a Patient.

Sometimes life presents us with challenges. In this case, my challenge was a forever, life change. My body image changed. I never flaunted my figure, nor did I ever use my body as a sexy forum but now I will never have that chance. The way I positioned myself to meet this challenge was by seeing it as forever healing, but this in itself was a challenge. I think times like this make you think about your whole life. What's good? What needs change? Who is important to you? Who treats you well? I have embraced my new image… I have worked hard to even "own" it. But, none of this was or is easy. Here's my flashback…

It was the middle of January and I had received grim news from my gastroenterologist. After a colonoscopy I was highly advised to consult a surgeon, not just any surgeon, but one of the best surgeons on the east coast. My sister and I went to the consultation appointment. After a lovely meet and greet, the surgeon asked, "What are your symptoms?" I replied, "I am good. I am managing. I have had Crohn's disease for almost 25 years. I live my life. I manage just fine." The surgeon replied, "Then why are you here?" I told him that my gastroenterologist had sent me here and I handed him a cd that contained images from a CT scan test. After a few looks, the surgeon left the room and requested another surgeon for a consult. The second surgeon asked, "What are your symptoms? Please be specific." "Ok… well…fevers daily, constant pressure, at times I feel a blockage and don't eat for twelve or so hours, but then it passes. I've lost an extensive amount of weight, but what girl would mind that…haha…the exhaustion I feel is only explained by a drained, lethargy that never goes away but, I go to work every day." Next, the surgeon says, "Please tell me about your lifestyle." I eagerly state, "I have two beautiful children, ages two and a half and seven months old…that I would never miss putting just one block on a tower with or not read a bedtime story to. I just finished my dissertation and earned a Doctoral degree last month and I am just a person who doesn't accept "pretty good" as an answer to anything in life, and I love my husband to death." "To me, every day is a gift." So again the first surgeon asks in a confused manner, "How do you live an active life with these symptoms?" I confidently reply, "The bottom line is that I refuse to be a patient because that's just not who I am. I have too many other things in life to enjoy and conquer! My whole life my doctors have been my friends. I do not define myself by my disease, rather I relish in personal goal setting and reaching goals." The surgeon sternly says, "Well without surgery, you will die."

The surgeons left the room to discuss. Initially they gave me one option: Go down stairs and sign into the emergency room. We will meet you down there and our team will perform a surgery tonight called a proctocolectomy with an end ileostomy. "Wait? What?" We will remove your entire colon and you will have "a bag." "Wait? What?" Tears poured down my face. I was only 32. I couldn't be in this position. I needed more options.

I was told that my colon could burst at any moment. My entire body would become septic. I could die. At that moment, I felt like I was in a dream. A very bad dream. My body became cold. Then I became frozen. I couldn't believe this was it. I heard nothing but my crying tears and the unclear echoes of others talking around me. The voices that surrounded me were droned out. I felt my sister's hand rest upon my arm and suddenly I felt like I came back to life.

Because I just couldn't make a life changing decision that fast, the surgeons scheduled me for an exploratory surgery that Friday. The promise was to explore laproscopically and see if any other options could be considered.

Friday came quickly. I remember looking at my children that morning. They were still sleeping. I walked into my son's room and watched him sleep in his red, corvette bed. He was two and a half years old. Love was shown in everything he did and everything he said. His world was so perfect…my husband and I made it this way. His laugh was contagious. If you looked closely in his eyes, you could always see peace and happiness. The joy he brought into my life was something I never could have imagined. In two and a half short years, he had become my little buddy. And then I walked in my daughter's room. Only seven months old, but her little personality was really starting to bud. The sparkle in her eyes came from her bold, happy cheeks that gently touched ear to ear. Her lovable hugs, kisses, and gestures kept me on my toes. I was more than satisfied with my life as a mom. A mom's love is something so unpredictable. I knew I would love my children, but the intensity of love that I have for both of them is immeasurable, and with each day only grew stronger. As I kissed my fingers and made the sign of the cross on each of their foreheads, I remember thinking…someone take care of them. Someone watch over them. And as naïve as it may sound, I was so scared that no one in the world could love them as much as I do and no one would take better care of them than me… and no one would advocate for them more than I would. It was never an option for me to be anywhere but beside them for the rest of my "long" life.

I was admitted into the hospital. I knew the risks of this were not totally avoidable; I may wake up with an ileostomy bag. My husband and sister walked me into the admission wing and waited while I changed into scrubs and handed them my belongings. I handed them everything I had on me, but in my head I remember thinking, "I'll hold on to my dignity." The IV went in…I was nervous to shut my eyes…thank goodness the medication did that for me. The vision of two angels, my children, were the last thing I could remember…

I woke up and flung my hand on my abdomen… nothing new. I was delighted and was overwhelmed with a strength that I could overcome this. Well, that quickly was taken from me when I was told the exploratory surgery was a failure. The surgeons were so taken back with what they saw that they did not want to go any further; touching anything internally could initiate an almost deadly situation.

I still was not ready to accept this surgery and life change…even though I knew I had no choice. But coming home to two beautiful children and being supported by my sister, husband and parents that evening was all I needed to confirm that the surgery was necessary. I have too much love in my heart to stop loving now…

The surgery was scheduled. I couldn't eat for three days prior to the surgery. By the third day I felt significantly weak, emotionally drained, and mentally "prepared." The night before my surgery my body crashed. After almost 25 years it was almost ready to give up… I passed out in my husband's arms…I remember going in and out of it and seeing my sister and husband standing in front of me. The love in my heart and the worry in their eyes brought me to consciousness.

The next morning there was a storm. Dark clouds. Snow. Bitter coldness…external factors supporting the misery of what February 5th would bring me. Complications during surgery were corrected immediately. Unforeseen challenges were successfully taken care of by the surgical teams. After a six hour surgery and recovery time… I awake. I am scared. I am still drugged! My sister and husband are there… I am safe.

February 2014, the Winter Olympics were on television in my hospital room. I watched for countless hours and I admired the athletic ability of many. But then I started to use an Olympic analogy of my own. Did I win the "gold?" I ran a Crohn's marathon for almost 25 years. Being diagnosed at eight years old isn't as hard as you may think because then you grow up not knowing any different. I never let this disease define what I did. I ran and ran. And now, did I finally cross the finish line?

Throughout a six day hospital stay my emotions shift from worry, fear, anxiety, and unrest to optimism, willingness, open-mindedness and a new appreciation for life. My life began to emerge. I was going to be ok. I was actually going to be better than ever.

As I was lying in my bed, I thought a lot about what was important in my life; I really appreciated the people that have and continue to surround me. I was amazed at my surprise visit from my uncle, overnight guests in the hospital, and my other visitors. But it wasn't only that week that people "showed up." I have never been a person who yearned for presents. Sometimes I think it's too easy – buy a gift, wrap, send. Instead I have noticed that the quality of my life actually emerged, not from what I had, but rather who "showed up." The quality of my life has always been determined by the people who surrounded me. Who showed up to hold my hand? Who showed up to take me to doctors? Who supported my ability to try new things? Who always showed up to my birthday parties, shows at school and graduations? Showing up is not always an easy thing to do. I don't remember all the tangible gifts that I have received over the years, but my heart holds a special place for all the family and friends who have shown up. This really helped me to work hard to heal and drove me to stay alive. To be honest though, recovery was not easy. Mentally and physically it was a challenge. Putting on a tough face for my children and husband wasn't always easy.

Months went by and my six month surgical anniversary came quickly. What a dramatic change for me! Physically, I never knew what I was missing. I have never felt this good or eaten this much. I now live energetically. And emotionally, I am healthier too. I care less about all the little petty things in life. When my life was on the line I knew what I wanted to live for, what I wanted in my life and what I would be missing if I were to die. My dear children, my loving husband, my amazing sister, my parents, all my family, my best friends, my fantastic job...the feelings of love, laughter and happiness...I didn't want to give those up and I actually had a hunger, a deep desire to learn more, enjoy more, travel more...and in turn: I worry less, stress less, care less about what others think, and life has become this beautiful gift that I am allowed to enjoy in a whole new way. Ok, so maybe I have this annoying bag, but it's a trade that is well worth the hassle. My image has changed, but I feel really lucky. Life is not something I take for granted. I did win the gold… my "gold." So glad internally and externally, I became a *New Beautiful!*

WHO AM I, NOT TO BE MYSELF?

I continually challenge myself to find out who I am because no one else can ever get into my mind and fully understand me, but me. There is no language in the world that can fully explain who we are. In some sense we live our lives partially alone. Alone in thought. Alone in feelings and emotions. But we must be confident. We must know ourselves. You must make choices for yourself, better your own life each moment. The past is not reality. It is gone. Every moment that passes is a moment lost – gone forever and never to be revisited, relived, or touched. Our future is untold, unwritten, and unknown. Therefore, all we have is the present. So what are we to do in each moment but live it. Live for the now. It is the only moment we have control over.

But don't live your life naively. Yes, it could be you. You could be the intelligent woman who loses a job, a spouse, a possession. You could be the woman who gets her identity stolen, whose house catches fire, whose car is stolen. But you may also be the woman whose values increase, whose husband adores you, and whose family is precious. Who are you not to be the woman who is fortunate? But I do guarantee that if you are the woman who looks in the mirror each day, able to take care of yourself, who is in control of her emotions, finances, and well being, then you are a strong woman who can live a life knowing that no one else fully knows who you are, but it doesn't matter, because you know yourself. You may identify yourself as a wife, as a daughter, as a friend...but no matter how you identify yourself, be confident...know who you truly are and be true to yourself. Life is each moment. You are to be who you are now. The past is gone. You are only living right now. Move forward. Make your own choices. Be confident.

Be a *New Beautiful*, whenever the time is right to change!

Be yourself, everyone else is taken.

THE UGLY DUCKLING

Beautiful, "pleasing the senses or mind aesthetically" (google.com). This word was never a term that I associated with myself. Growing up I was always known as the "fat kid." My family and friends found many ways to let me know that I was not very good at "pleasing the senses or mind aesthetically." My nickname in kindergarten was "Canoli," my grandmother used to call me cavallo (horse in Italian) and my grandfather's best friend used to kindly refer to me as "faccia bruta" (ugly face). As a child and pre-teen I never felt beautiful. I never even felt pretty. I was basically ostracized on so many levels because of my appearance. As a result of this, I grew up without any self-confidence or self-worth. It's very difficult being the odd man out. You can't understand why people don't see you for who you are on the inside, why they only care about the appearance on the outside.

When I got to college I became obsessed with my appearance. I wanted desperately to fit in and be accepted. I began to work out, buy nice clothes, put on decent make-up and style my hair in a more fashionable manner. I started to notice that it was working. Underneath all the awkwardness there was actually a pretty face that I was able to bring out. So, for a while this really made me feel better. I felt like I could finally be accepted. I thought that maybe I had finally found my place.

Ironically, I began to notice that it was having the opposite effect. My friends didn't like the fact that now I was getting the attention, that now the "hot" guys were paying attention to me. Everyone knows that every group of girls has that one ugly friend. The one that just can't get it right no matter what she does, but deep down tries so very hard to fit in. I had been that person for years, but once that began to change, they didn't like or appreciate that the wave of attention shifted. Eventually I just wanted to crawl into a hole. No matter what I did I couldn't win. Either I was too ugly or too pretty. I started to really question if there was something wrong with me. Why couldn't I just get it right? I began to live every day like a robot. I pretended to be happy and confident on the outside but on the inside I was a mess. More like a disaster if I'm going to be completely honest with myself. I couldn't find an inner peace and just be happy with ME. Who was I supposed to be…the ugly duckling or the swan?

Then the unimaginable happened, I met my husband. We dated for a while and eventually got engaged. For the first time in my life I actually felt like someone loved me for who I truly was. I felt loved on the inside and on the outside. There truly is no better feeling in the world. Life was good…life was beautiful. Except that in the middle of all this my mom got really sick. She was diagnosed with Pulmonary Hypertension a few years before and things were just starting to worsen. Just when I thought life was positively changing, I was becoming the swan; life was becoming beautiful; my whole world came crashing down.

My mother passed away 2 months before my wedding. Two months before what was supposed to be the happiest day of my life. April 19, 2006 rocked my world in a way I never thought possible. I had never experienced such feelings of loss or pain. The irony in all this is that my mother and I had never been close while I was growing up. I think it was that we were so similar and it caused us to butt heads a lot. It wasn't until I got engaged that things really started to change. Planning the wedding and making all of the arrangements brought us closer than we had ever been; closer than I could have ever dreamed of. I worked hard to plan it so we could get married within the year. I wouldn't admit it out loud, but deep down in my soul I knew we didn't have much time left with her. I so desperately wanted her to at least be able to see one of her daughters get married.

One of the most vivid memories is from when she was in the hospital. My father, fiancée, and I had driven in to see her. We spent a few lovely hours just chatting and enjoying each other's company. When it came time to leave I remember having this weird feeling and just not wanting to leave her. Something kept stopping me from walking out that door. Before I walked out, I remember turning around and seeing her with her head in her hand sobbing. She said "I just want to see my children get married and meet my grandchildren." That moment broke me; it broke me into a million pieces because I knew that it would never happen. She never did get to see any of her daughters get married. She never did get to meet any of her grandchildren. She died a few months later. I didn't feel very beautiful at that time. I felt ugly, hurt, lost, and defeated. It seemed like I could never really get to a beautiful place and stay there.

After my mom died everyone wanted me to postpone my wedding. "Wait and give it time." But I couldn't wait. I had to do it. I wanted to get married, not just for my husband and myself, but for my mom too.

The anticipation of the day brought us closer than I could have ever imagined. The wedding gave us the mother/daughter relationship that I had always dreamed of. But, most importantly it made her fight. I knew it gave her a will to live, something to make her want to keep going.

So on June 17, 2006 I walked down the aisle looking beautiful for my mother. I decided that from that day on I would always be beautiful no matter what. I had finally found my *"New Beautiful."* I want my mother to be proud of me every time she looks down on me. I want to be the woman she was and more. I finally figured out that it didn't matter what I looked like or what people thought of me, I just wanted to be a good person. I finally found my beautiful just being the woman I know my mother would want me to be. I decided to stop caring so much about what people thought and just started doing things that made me happy, things that would make her happy. This is what finally transformed me from the ugly duckling into the swan.

The years following my wedding were not easy. To this day I can still see her sitting in that hospital bed wearing her pink pajamas and sobbing into her hands. I was there the day she died, watched her slip away, but that day at the hospital is the day that still stays with me. Strangely enough it's the image that keeps me going every day. Whenever I'm down, or I'm feeling ugly, or I feel like giving up, I remember what my mother had to give up and I live my life for her. I live every day trying to be kind, hardworking, understanding, devoted to my friends and family and a positive role model to my students. I fight all my inner demons every day to be a NEW BEAUTIFUL for my mother. My mother who at 50 years young died BEAUTIFUL!

When I redefined beauty...I became a *New Beautiful*!

MY OWN
BEAUTIFUL PATH

The deafening sound of the phone receiver slamming down was unmistakable! My father's reaction to the decision I had just informed him of was clearly understood. At that moment, I did not know if I would ever see or speak with him or my mother again, but I knew that I had just taken a major step in forever changing my life. How my life was going to change was unclear at the time; however, a change had been made nevertheless. Despite my parents' steadfast refusal to accept my decision to marry someone outside my culture, I was determined to do so and eloped. I had finally asserted myself in a way that shocked me more than it did them. Where did the courage or audacity as others may perceive it, to defy not only my parents but cultural norms that had existed in my family for many, many generations come from? After all, disobeying one's family in many parts of the Middle East could cost a woman her life. My parents' dismay, I am certain, did not only stem from the fact that I had overtly defied them, but also from the fact that I had always been a fairly obedient child. Other than occasional outbursts typical of young people, I pretty much behaved in ways that were expected of me but often left me feeling completely suffocated. As a child and later as a young woman, I could not articulate feeling isolated, somewhat oppressed, and as though I needed to be someone other than myself to be accepted. Nevertheless, not expressing these feelings out loud did not lessen them. In fact, the older I became, the more intense these feelings became.

Looking back on that time in my life, I do not believe I was left with much of a choice but to blatantly disregard my family's wishes and plans for my life. My parents, I am certain, could not understand how I could have done this to them. How could I have rebelled against them in such an unimaginable way? I, on the other hand, could not understand how they could not see it coming. After all, when I had gone to them to tell them I wanted to marry Andrew, instead of supporting me or taking the time to get to know him, they forbade me from seeing him. The distance and resentment between my parents and myself only grew worse as I told them that they could not keep me from seeing or marrying him. They were obstinate about their decisions, and I was equally adamant about mine. I began to come home from work later and later to avoid the constant arguments with my mother, while my father completely stopped speaking to me for a brief while. After two months of this almost daily battle, causing me to feel further isolated and alone, I finally made the decision that my life would no longer be dictated by other people. I came to the realization that in order for me to create the life that I wanted for myself, I could no longer allow others to impose their decisions on me, nor to place limits on what I could achieve.

I began to question whether or not I was sending messages to others that I was incapable of making my own decisions and that it was incumbent upon them to them to tell me what I could and could not do. Was there something written on my forehead that offered these people the presumption to attempt to tell me what I was and was not capable of achieving? Take, for example, the time an educator informed me that no one would hire me as a teacher because I was very shy and introverted. At that time in my life, I was a student teacher and very excited about the prospect of having my own class. What this teacher failed to realize was that despite my shyness, I felt tremendously comfortable working with children and that it had been a life-long dream of mine to become a teacher. Although her comments upset and caused me to temporarily doubt myself, I became more determined to prove her wrong. Within a few months of graduating from college, I was offered and accepted a full-time teaching position. This experience taught me that no one can place limits on your accomplishments unless you allow them.

At a very young age, I recall having an unwavering passion and perseverance to accomplish what others considered unattainable. Where did this drive to succeed come from? After all, I was a little girl growing up in the war-infested, West Bank where women married young and became wives and mothers. Even the Arab women that obtained an education eventually succumbed to the cultural expectations set for them. I remember sitting with my mother on the landing of the many steps that led from our house to the streets and watching her, as I had done so many times before, peeling an orange in one continuous turn. I was five or six years of age at that time. My mother always fed fruit after dinner to my nine siblings and me, and to this day I still prefer a juicy apple or sweet peach over a piece of cake. As my mother was skillfully removing the skin of another orange, I saw our neighbor who lived up the hill from us walk past her front door. As expected, she was pregnant once again. I believe this was her fifth child. As I looked up at this neighbor, I was suddenly filled with a life prediction that, "…That would never be me." Without realizing it, I had spoken those words out loud. The look of sheer horror and confusion on my mother's face is as clear to me today at the age of 49 as it was almost 44 years ago. After her mouth gaped open and she finally found the words to speak, she asked me what I meant by that statement. I told her that I was going to become a teacher and that I wanted more out of life than to be pregnant and raise ten children, as was my mother's fate. My mother stared at me, once more, and told me that I shouldn't dream such outrageous dreams, as getting married and having children was the expectation for Arab women at that time. This was surprising to me as my mother always taught my siblings and me that education was important. For my sisters and me, however, she always spoke about us becoming educated as a "back-up plan," meaning that we should use our education if our husband unexpectedly dies or becomes disabled. She did not discuss it as a life-long passion and for us to become completely independent; it was to be used in the event we needed to rely on it.

Looking back on that day, I still cannot figure out where that revelation came from, but I knew that somehow, some way, I needed to make it a reality. Little did I know then that at the age of ten I would be immigrating to America with my family and eventually finding myself living a life whose path I chose (or maybe it chose me), filled with decisions that were mostly my own. That road, however, was far beyond a smooth one. It was filled with bumps, blinding curves and, at times, tremendous pain and heartache.

At the age of twenty-three, I made the drastic decision to elope and that forever changed the course of my life. Although I could not predict at that time what my future would hold and the price that decision would cost me, I chose a trail that is filled with zero remorse and one that I will always treasure.

As I look back on that cold, blustery January day in 1989, I am reminded of Janet Jackson's song "Control." Like

Janet, I had been aching to take control of my own life. I truly loved Andrew and could not understand why it was wrong of me to want to marry him, despite the fact that he was from a different culture. The decisions that were being made for me by my family did not suit me, but I was stuck in a cultural rut. A hunger had existed in me as far back as I can remember to seek knowledge, to be independent, to explore, and to correct the double standards that existed in my family and culture for males and females. However, the messages I consistently received at home always caused me to struggle between what I wanted out of life and what I had been taught were the appropriate choices for me. Little did I know then of the impact this decision was going to have upon my life and the life of my sisters. Growing up in a home where my father and five brothers were dominant figures, and my mother, four sisters and I the submissive others, I believe that I had changed the course of my family's history and beliefs by eloping.

That day marked the beginning of the new me and allowed me to pave the way for my sisters to also make their own decisions. Of course, they had each also fought these double standards in their own ways, but my decision, I believe, had been the most drastic as I was the first of the daughters to marry. Not surprisingly, three of my four sisters have married men outside of our culture with little resistance from the family. In fact, two of the three of them are divorced with one on her second marriage. The courage that it took for me to challenge cultural norms provided me with the strength to seek and accomplish more goals and dreams. Since that time, I have continued to not only make my own decisions but to further test and resist those cultural beliefs.

I divorced my first husband and married someone else outside of my culture, and have moved up the ladder of success to hold a position in education on Long Island that was once also dominated by males. These decisions have all gone against what I had been raised to believe about myself as a woman. Some members of my family have learned to accept me for the person that I am, while others grew further and further away from me. The latter ones, I believe, remain bewildered as to what I might do next or just do not know how to connect with me and I with them. At the present time in my life, I have a closer relationship with the youngest three of my five brothers. I love and respect them tremendously as they are honest, hard-working men who are devoted husbands and fathers and who recognize and appreciate my accomplishments, and I theirs. As for my sisters, they are equally independent women who have also chosen their own life and career paths. We love and support one another through good and challenging times.

My first marriage did not work out and, in fact, lasted for a very brief period of time. Consequently, I learned so many *beautiful* lessons from the experiences surrounding my decisions to elope, have a traditional wedding, and subsequently divorce. One of the many lessons I learned was that it was very important for me to surround myself with people who accepted me for ME! I especially learned that a man had to earn the right to be in my life. This included brothers and other male relatives, as well as male friends. They needed to be respectful, supportive, non-judgmental, caring and, most importantly, accept me for who I am without trying to control me.

Because of these revelations, I was ready for the right man when my husband entered my life 23 years ago. He proved to be loving, caring, respectful of women, and would not hinder me in my professional endeavors. In fact, he has always supported and encouraged me in pursuing my goals.

The experiences of leaving and divorcing Andrew helped me to find the strength I did not previously recognize existed in me. Unbeknownst to me at the time, living on my own for the first time in my life was a blessing in disguise in that it forced me to dig deeper within myself and to soul search. The realization that I had taken myself out of one male dominant situation to another with Andrew was certainly an eye opening moment for me. I became keenly aware of the qualities of the life I wanted for myself, the person I wanted to be, and the people with whom I would surround myself. The level of gratitude I have for the painful experiences surrounding my divorce is tremendously high as they have helped to shape me into the strong, independent, and determined woman I am today. These characteristics have not only been crucial to me personally as I have had to live through heartaches and unexpected tragedies, but they have been equally important in my professional life.

Being one of the first Arab-American females in a district, leadership position, couldn't have happened without tremendous strength, perseverance, and a strong sense of self-awareness. My prior personal experiences, undoubtedly, helped to contribute to my professional successes.

My past experiences have also taught me that I had the choice to behave either as a mistreated woman or a triumphant one. I could choose to walk around like a victim or use my experiences to help me gain a better perspective of myself and, therefore, take a more active role in my own life. The latter choice helped me to grow and to recognize that difficult life experiences can be viewed as a vehicle to a higher level of self-awareness.

Occasionally, as I reflect upon the day I chose to make my life decisions my own, I ask myself whether or not I had gained my independence in the proper way. The answer is always the same…"Absolutely!" I truly believe that had I not fought with full force against my family's and first husband's cultural and male-dominant standards, the outcomes would have been different for me. Although at the time it was not my intent, I hope that I have become a role model for other female Arabic women living in male-dominant homes who also want to choose their own life paths, both personally and professionally.

Several years later, my parents and I formed closer relationships than, I believe, we had previously experienced. They finally saw me as an independent adult who was capable of making her own decisions and one that accepted the rewards or consequences of those decisions. Our relationship became one that was not only based on love but also on respect and acceptance. They recognized that our cultural beliefs could not remain fully intact, while trying to assimilate into the American culture.

My parents were two of the most loving, compassionate, and intelligent people who were fully committed to their ten children. As a young adult, I could not understand how two such adoring people were so opposed to me marrying someone from a different cultural background.

What I learned later, however, was that my parents' decisions were not based on prejudice or lack of respect for other cultures; instead, they were desperately trying to preserve our own culture because it was one that was familiar and comfortable for them. Since they were immersed in our culture, they did not know how to let go of its expectations. As I became happier in my life and more successful in my professional pursuits, they learned to let go of some cultural norms, especially those that did not necessarily empower women. They were very proud of their children and their individual accomplishments.

In May 2003, I graduated with my Doctorate in Education and Administration. As we left the graduation, I noticed that my Dad walked out of the ceremony with 25-30 copies of the program. At the time, I could not understand his purpose for these multiple copies. A couple of weeks later, I learned that he and my Mom had distributed these copies to many parishioners within our church and customers who frequented his grocery store. Any doubts about my life decisions that I may have had at the time were immediately dismissed when I learned of his reasoning.

Both of my parents passed away within the past few years. Despite the hardships that we faced together and the loss of time battling our own cultural fights, my parents and I grew to have a very close and loving relationship. Greater parents, in my opinion, do not exist and I will forever be grateful to them for helping me to challenge expectations and to achieve confidence and exuberance for life that I may not otherwise have gained.

If I could go back in time, I would not change a thing. Although some of my decisions led me to travel down a bumpier road, they have been my own decisions. Having choice is a privilege for which I have fought long and hard, and it is my hope to empower other women to also fight for this right. By making confident, independent choices, I became a *New Beautiful*.

YOUR WORDS HIT
ME LIKE KNIVES

I was in a relationship that was so positive, so alive, full of happiness…and then became dismissive. But I went with it. I kept hanging on. I kept trying. But with every effort placed into the repair, more damage was continually hurting me. I could question my actions. I could reflect and think I was wrong, but I would just be angered with myself. It was time to heal. Time to move on but also it was a time to personally and emotionally grow. The healing process began and in the end, a *New Beautiful.* Here is the poem I wrote while healing:

Your words hit me like knives, piercing my heart
over and over again.
Why do you treat me this way?
And why do I accept it?
You have emotionally scarred my insides.

Your words and actions are toxic.

You pierce me down to the bone with your sharp words,

tore apart my heart, leaving pieces scattered from your conscious, negative decisions.

You have melted my trust away with your heated discussions with another…

And consequently, the silence of your words, the absence of your actions are pure torture…more painful, more confusing…

And why am I here? But where am I? Where is here?

Where is home anymore?

Laying in bed without you is painful.

Memories flood back like nightmares from the past.

Hoping to forget these black, death memories,

they surface like a poisonous resurrection.

Who are you, when you become lost from yourself?

Who are you when you look in the mirror?

Why did you leave your generous, loving soul to live in a shell of yourself?

You are empty and cannot fill the void you look for.

You will soon be left alone.

Do not stop to turn around and see me gone.

You will know I am gone when your heart aches and your loneliness accrues…

You will know I am gone when your heart feels death.

You will know I am gone when you look around,

and feel like a stranger.

Because your life as you know it will be a distant memory… Soon the pulse from your heart will only beat to survive because I will not be here for you to love…

Divorce…It's a new start…*a New Beautiful.*

LIFE

"You are what you eat!" "Always be thankful!" "No one is here to make you happy...you have to find that within." "One day we will find that the sun is bad for our skin!" - Mom

Several phrases of encouragement that I heard many times throughout the years!

At 55 years young, I could not imagine how "right on" my mother's pontificating was. As I sit here writing, on a snowy, winter's day, I take note of a plump red cardinal, sitting in my birdbath, eating seeds with beauty and grace. Such visual beauty! I remark on how happy and content I am. "The small things... Joy!"

Our life journey often takes turns...up, down, zigzag and all around! Sometimes this journey often takes us on a different path from what we had planned. At first, the detour is a shock, it is upsetting and we feel lost, but then our eyes and heart readjust and we learn we are not living just for ourselves, but for those close to us and to whom we love and cherish. We have to make peace within our inner selves and find strength to move in the new direction, and to make new plans within our new path. "When a door closes, another opens."

The true beauty of age is to look back with a clarity of mind and to acknowledge that some of our defining moments are teaching moments and that adversity gives us a chance to build up, do better and to create an opportunity for change and something new. Don't let the detour throw you off track or define the rest of your life, let it be a new path to something wonderful. Choose life and make it a happy, fun one. Always be open and receiving to your experiences…good and bad. The test is there, but the results are yours. Own it and run with it…feel your life! Life, in and of itself…has made me a *New Beautiful*.

Renaming Myself

I believe in love and happiness! I believe these two things fill my heart and give me intrinsic drive every day to do good things, set professional and personal goals, and this has become the framework for all I do. So to sum up my life– I want to love with all my heart and be loved in return. And I want to be happy each day with all the people I interact with and be happy wherever I am: at home, at work,… simple goals --- right? Normal things all people strive for?!

Well let's be real - I can't - no one can probably have love and happiness consume them all day, every day - so my choice and life philosophy is: "Feel love, be loved and be happy as much as you can and when you're not feeling those things - work really hard to get back to a place in life when you can fill your heart with love and happiness."

Throughout my life, I have realized the quality of each day is naturally different. One day you are enjoying life and laughing…and the next you become stressed, frustrated, and angry. Emotions are part of being human. Being self-reflective helped me to realize when I was living in an illusion of happiness and I needed to get out of it. As I went through all of the "emotions of divorce," I kept a journal and looking back I want to share my journey to happiness with other women. Now some women may choose to blame their ex-spouse, and although I could write about that, I chose to focus on how I took control of my life and owned my character. This chapter isn't about him. Through reflection, I focused on who I was and prepared for who I wanted to be in order to set up a happy and loving future...

So looking back...I was happily married for a couple of years. My husband and I just closed on a new house. When you look for a house and see physical space, beautiful landscaping, a good community and a prosperous school district, you imagine a great future. You also emotionally imagine a "happy" life, "happy" kids and a loving home. At that time, I loved my "potential life." My future seemed ideal, fairytale like. I didn't need all the bells and whistles because to me life was perfect.

When I signed all the paperwork at the house closing a sense of peace overtook me. I had reached a point in my life that for years I had dreamed of: I married my best friend, had a career, saved money, and bought a home. And to seem even more perfect, we moved into our new home one week before Christmas. So we quickly put up a 2 ft. tree with decorations and prepared to celebrate. Champagne was popped and a genuine love and happiness filled my heart.

But a few weeks later, I first caught my husband texting with another woman, "just a co-worker." We spoke about it. He denied anything more than a friendship and we moved on. Then it continued. But again, reassured me it was nothing. A couple of months later, I saw some text message conversations. "Wish we could talk, but I know your wife is home." Fear penetrated my heart and my mind continued to have a dark, heavy thought that consumed me each day… Could this be true?!

I overheard a conversation with him and her on the phone…It was real this time…I just couldn't believe it. Although I expected life to never be the same, it took a turn in a dramatic way…a turn I never saw coming. One morning, two months later, I woke up, showered, had coffee and went to work. Just a normal Friday morning. My husband woke up, showered, got dressed and went to "work." Just a normal Friday morning. The difference was coming home to a half empty house. My husband had left.

I became…Mrs. Shock

I walked through the house. Over and over. What was taken? What was still here? Our new car – gone. Our computer – gone. A flash drive was left on the kitchen counter. My files were on the flash drive and half of the money was left in our accounts for me. Closets half empty. Looking at my bed, I remember that there were only pillows on my side. The two bedrooms on the second floor were being renovated and all the tools were taken. I remember looking at those bare walls. All that was standing were the beams, and the insides were empty. That's just how I felt… empty. But I was thinking, "How am I going to complete this project?" The cell phone charger – gone. With every turn of each corner in my house – I remember seeing so many missing things. Turning and twisting and walking in and out of each room, it felt like hours. Why did I keep looking? Why did it matter what was taken? I'm not sure, but at that moment it just did. My jaw hung low, but not lower than my heart felt. Tears poured down my face so rapidly, for so long, that I think I eventually dried up and became numb. Oh - my wedding picture still hung. The pictures of the two of us stood untouched. All the happy memories stayed intact. Not moved. Not taken - not even thought about, I assumed.

My cell phone rang. I ran over to pick it up immediately. It was him! He must have made a mistake. But after a very short conversation with my husband, I only learned that he was safe and that supposedly I did nothing wrong. How could I do nothing wrong, but my world be turned upside down? No one asked if I wanted this to happen to me? How I didn't fall to the floor with shock still amazes me to this day. But as I was listening and hearing the words, I was so empty inside. The words seemed to echo throughout my hollow body. My reply to him on the phone was "Are you ok?" How could I be so kind to even ask or care? But I know I really did care. I was really concerned. I really loved him.

Two of my dear friends were called and ran over. They listened. They hugged me. They were just as shocked as I was. We drank wine. I needed that. We laughed. I tried to forget. I will never be able to thank them enough for that night. It was just what I needed.

The night was almost over. We were all tired. I took out the garbage… and then I ran. I ran so far…blocks and blocks. I had never run before in my life. Why now? I still don't know. I guess I was trying to escape something but I really could have run all night and still never would have found what I was emotionally looking for.

The next morning I called my father and asked him to come over and talk. As he walked in the door, a sense of calmness took over. My father has always been a hero of mine. Probably top on my list! And so I said, "My husband left me." His faced looked like he had seen a ghost. He hugged me. I will never forget the warm, loving, "I'm here for you" kind of hug. We sat on the couch and the first words he said to me were, "I am so glad for you." "What?" I stood there in deep confusion. My father continued, "I always wanted for you and your sister to grow up and be in control of your own life. You have a profession and make enough money to make your own choices. The ball is in your court." *I always kept that conversation in the back of my head…*

However, Mrs. Shock wanted to work on it because, this *can't really be happening.* So I slowly shifted into a new identity.

I became…Mrs. Fix-it.

To protect myself, I went to the bank and secured my half of the money. I changed all my passwords on my accounts.

But then it hit me. I needed to work on this. I know I could "fix-it." I began to think with my heart and no longer my head. I began living in the past. I actually started talking of my husband as if he had two personalities, "Old Nick. New Nick." The old Nick I knew was just amazing. So loving, so kind. We were best friends. We drank together. Played games together. Laughed together. Took trips together. We were a great team. But then the "New Nick" emerged. I couldn't even recognize him. The songs he listened to on the radio changed. The taste of food for him even changed. And one time I remember a friend being over and she cursed. He turned around, so serious and somber and said something like, "Please don't use foul language in front of me." My friend and I looked at each other – as if our eyes were asking, "Who is this?" I knew I needed to help. Was my husband was going through some type of identity crisis? Maybe settling down in one place? Maybe our new home wasn't something he wanted? Maybe settling down triggered something emotional and now he is in depression or having an identity crisis. There were so many questions and just no answers. Well, I liked living in the past and not really ready to acknowledge the present, so I tried. I tried really hard. I went to counseling. I lived alone in our new house. It was clear that this issue he was going through was quite traumatic. So I needed to help. I did whatever he wanted. Some days he wouldn't call. I would cry. But I would wait. Days might go by, but my phone stayed charged and on the highest volume setting. When we did speak, I would be elated. Each night we didn't, I cried myself to sleep.

I tried so hard to support him and was glad he was getting "time alone to think." The nights he wanted to stop by the house, I would make myself available. Sometimes we even met for dinner. I would continually ask, "What are the problems? What can I do?" He called all the shots and I tried to continually support him. The blame game was something I wanted to do. I was determined that if he could state a problem, I could try to fix it. The illusion of our relationship grew stronger. Then another shift happened.

I became...Mrs. Phony.

We were ok. I knew that we were going to be ok. We went to events together. We were even both in a bridal party for our two best friends. We danced. We drank. We had a great time. The summer neared and I convinced my husband to work at the same place I was working. With much hesitation, he agreed. That year the summer was long: nights spent alone, taking care of my new house, cleaning, bills, landscaping, and the construction project upstairs. For a few months, my father would come over on the weekends and we would work: we fixed and upgraded the electricity, hung sheetrock, painted, bought new rugs and finalized the molding. And out of nowhere – SURPRISE! My husband would sleep at home again... here and there...maybe a couple times a week. I think this was the epitome of my denial. I was ok. I could move forward with all my future plans. But this place of "phony" was not something that lasted. I was too good for this. I didn't want to live in a lie, nor did I want to define myself as a woman who lacked all control. I didn't want to be a wife whose husband chose on a daily basis whether or not he wanted to see her, live with her, or talk to her. How did this fantasy I was living in become crushed and rearranged?! I knew it was time I accepted the fact that I didn't have to be emotionally abused anymore.

So I became…Mrs. Sleuth.

Things just didn't add up. No longer was it ok for me to feel and live this way. I am not the smartest woman in the world, but I also know when I am being lied to. No longer was it ok for me to be treated so poorly, like a doormat or worse – be disrespected and appeared to be a fool. As I started gathering information reality started to kick in. All the text messages?! Analyzing the monthly cell phone minute usages only added to my disappointment, and upset. Why wasn't I the one being called? Who else can care and love him the way I do? There were new forms of social media that had just launched, making it easy to publically access information, pictures, and posts. My friend had come to me with pictures that disturbed me. I guess pictures don't lie. But they do paint awful pictures in your head that not even an artist's eraser can take away. I was cleaning the garage and found a cell phone, under a blanket on a charger. Why is there another phone that I didn't know about charging in my own garage? Thoughts raced through my head. Anyway, I had more and more evidence to prove the point of dishonesty…but I wouldn't stop looking. What piece of evidence would make me file for divorce? Leave him?

I just kept searching… Ironically, I think at this point, on this emotional rollercoaster, I was actually looking for a piece of evidence that proved me wrong. But I just couldn't find one. I wanted an answer. I wanted to be the problem. But time after time, my husband said it was all him. It was nothing I had directly done. I continued to be a detective, over and over again. And what did I do with this all?

I became… Mrs. Avoidance.

I kept holding on. I knew the truth. But I wanted "one more holiday" "one more date" "one more fun night out." I knew what I had to do, but I kept avoiding calling a lawyer. I wanted to give him more time. More time to realize he was wrong. More time to say "I'm sorry." But mostly, I wanted to give him more time to go back to the old person I knew… the person I fell in love with…the man that took care of me, loved me, and was a person of loyalty and respect.

Well the time finally came. I knew I wasn't truly happy… I still had snapshots of happiness with him, usually when other people were around or at work. But at home, when I was all alone with him, I knew I wasn't truly happy.

I became…Mrs. Toxic.

I knew the life I was living was not satisfying me. I wanted so much more out of life. I wanted to feel loved. I wanted to feel respected. The emotional games were playing with my mind and heart. I watched the strong character of my family never wither. My parents forgave. My sister and friends welcomed him back into their lives. But as everyone around me tried to support what I *thought* I wanted, my insides began to warp. I was distraught and being destroyed. I am a genuine person and living a life like this was toxic for me. I wasn't physically alone, but I realized that I was emotionally alone for months now. I flash back to what my father said about being glad for me. I knew I should be glad for me too. The next step for me was going to be a huge shift. It was a shift from a feeling of Mrs. to a feeling of "Ms."

I became...**MS.** Action.

I called a lawyer. I cried. I gathered all my paperwork and my checkbook. I made an appointment. It was time. I remember the lawyer stating, "Why are you really here?" My response, "I am ready to change my life. I am ready to work towards happiness." I was functioning quite well at work. I was in pursuit of my doctoral degree. I was managing a household basically on my own. I even was growing a vegetable garden! As my inner strength grew stronger and I continually had so much support from my family and best friends, I realized I was going to be ok. I was actually going to be better than ever.

I became...Ms. Self Preservation and on a quest to be Ms. Happiness.

Now, I want to be honest, I felt like the table was turning. I decided that I was not letting my husband call all the shots. I started making plans and keeping them whether he was home or not. I started to decorate the house and do the things I wanted to do. Slowly, it didn't matter what his schedule looked like because I had my own to worry about. I never lowered my standards to meet his, but I did raise my expectations for myself as a confident, independent woman!

I quickly became…Ms. In-Control.

Realizing my actions were not dependent upon his, I liked the idea that my future was mine. I wrote a letter to give to my husband to accompany the letter my lawyer drew up, specifying that he needed representation and that a legal separation was in progress. My letter was more about choices. To be honest, I was gaining confidence, but honestly, I still was not 100% ready to give up on the marriage. I am not sure if this was the real case or I just was teasing him, but I know that my mind was not completely made up. However, I was ready to be in a place where I was strictly looking out for myself. Here are some lines from the letter I wrote him:

> I don't think I will fully understand what happened. I don't know why you chose to do the things you did. I will never understand who or what steered you so far from the person I once knew. No one is perfect, but you were to me. I held you on the highest pedestal. Sometimes it seems as though you are a stranger to me.
>
> We all make choices in life. We become the people we want to become. We make choices to drive our lives in the directions we want to go. I think life is supposed to be fun, happy, and filled with successes… successes that we have set goals for and have achieved. I am a person too. You had made

so many choices in the last nine months, choices that, at times, I have not understood at all. You have chosen to hurt me over and over. You chose to have secrets, live in a separate place, and basically live a separate life in which I have not been included. These things emotionally beat me up.

This letter helped me gain control and become…Ms. Detachment. And so…He finally moved back into "our" house permanently; <u>however</u> a week later, I moved out. Two of my best friends, kindly opened their home to me. They invited me to live in their basement and showed kindness that I could never express in words. Not only did they offer me a nothing-type of rent deal, because I was still paying half the mortgage on my home, I would come home to dinner on the table, laughs, hugs, and conversation. These became consistent parts of my day. I was so glad to have happiness at "home" on a daily basis again. I looked forward to seeing them at the end of each day.

I knew what I wanted in life. I wanted respect. I wanted honesty and loyalty. I wanted to feel true love. I wanted to be intellectually stimulated. I wanted to laugh until my stomach hurt. I wanted to be happy. Those things I believe I deserved, and didn't want to live without any longer.

I know we all have to make choices. But the best ones, the most important ones are the choices we have to make for ourselves. Sometimes being selfish is mandatory. So I realized that detaching from him, actually wasn't about him, it was about me.

I needed to become…Ms. Fabulous.

I was only 27 years old. I had a life to live. I knew I couldn't fully forgive my husband for all of the lies and all of the heartache. So it wasn't fair to either of us to continue this marriage. I had so many amazing friends, a loving, supporting family, and best of all, I knew after this fall, I would land on my feet. I knew I could take care of myself and I was happy. I had a great job. I was fabulous! On the forefront of my mind was the definition of who I wanted to be and I had to act on that to become that person. I was honest with myself and although the decision to finalize a divorce wasn't easy.

It made me become…Ms. Liberated!

The day I had to sign the papers, my journal reads:

> *I return to the notion that in life we all have control to create our own happiness. I sat for 2 hours in a small attorney's office. While examining a 36 page agreement, I felt like my life was divided into compartmental categories, analyzed to death and belittled into words. How could the most important parts of my life be reified into written words?*

As I sat there and gained my independence, agreeing to surrender my rights to my husband's retirement, life insurance, 401K, and, enhanced earning. The "flip of the coin" was that I was gaining my freedom and gaining the sole rights to my own earnings, property, retirement, savings and investments. Realizing that I wasn't getting anything handed to me—all of the financial parts of the agreement that were "mine" were earned. My life is how it is because I made it this way.

How do we break down and describe our own life? Can it be done? We can try; however I believe some of the most important things in life are feelings and cannot be fully measured or fully described by someone else.

As I signed and initialized the last document, my chest tightened. I stopped and thought about this moment being the last moment in this particular chapter in my life. I breathed. I knew this is what I needed to do. I was confident. Happy, warm memories remained in my heart. I would only be the person I am now because of my life experiences.

Life happens constantly, we cannot slow it down, stop or pause it. But we can enjoy it! We can embrace it! We can learn from it! And most of all, we can create happiness and feel love within it. And so six years later… who am I now?

I became … Dr. Mom.

I finished my doctoral degree in the education field. I also finished a school building and district administration program. But that's not what makes me so happy. I had major surgery that basically cured a chronic disease, bought a new, amazing house, but yet still that is not what fills my heart with love and happiness. I met the man who compliments me, completes me and makes me laugh. Together, our love created two perfect children. The four of us, *my family* that is what makes me so happy. And as I said earlier – sometimes life just happens, but by making confident choices and paving a successful life path for ourselves, we inevitably create our own happiness.

Life is about choices. As I look back and think about all the difficult emotional and financial choices I had to make. I realize that I made those choices because I knew I wanted something more. And what I have now, my family, is a priceless gift that I never could have dreamed up. How blessed I am to be so happy, so genuinely happy and loved!

By working through these stages of my life…I became a *New Beautiful*.

A SPECIAL APPRECIATION FOR LIFE

One day I was sitting and thinking about my life. I thought about all the challenges that I have faced and I thought about what I would answer if someone asked me, "What made you the person you are today?" First, I would have to answer that the love and faith from my family and friends shaped my whole life. My husband and my daughters have fulfilled my dreams in so many ways. Thirty years ago, I lost my mom, whom I was so close to. But her love has always stayed with me. I had to carry her love with me to guide me! And another huge factor that has defined me is my job. All of the students I have worked with inspired me and changed my life for the better!

Since I was in third grade, my dream was to become a wife, mother and teacher. I knew from that young age I wanted to work with children. I became a teacher's assistant in 1997 for a nursery school for many years, then for a public elementary school for six years and now for three years I have worked in a high school. I currently work with sixteen to twenty-one year olds with special needs.

My day starts with the Life Skills Program and Job Training. Then for the rest of the day, I work one on one in a self contained class. I love all of my students. Their challenges can go from learning how to communicate, express feelings to understanding careers, writing checks, math facts, etc…I look up to them! Their challenges can be everyday things that we all take for granted.

The young adults that I work with inspire me and make me a better person. I think they help me more than I help them. It's a two way street. Their challenges are a lot harder than many of ours. Their priorities are certainly in order. Do they ask for a new car, new shoes, or expensive jewelry? No, not really. They ask to be accepted, validated, loved, and understood. Don't we all really need that? When I think about complaining, I stop and think about how some people have trouble on a daily basis doing things that can be considered basic. Of course, I am not an expert and I am simply stating my feelings from my experiences and from my heart! But this makes me realize how trivial day to day life stresses can be. And I have learned to truly define the real "challenges" in my life.

I truly feel blessed to have met, loved and worked with so many beautiful and amazing students in my career. Children are our future. We should love and nurture them not demean or destroy their confidence. Children are the true heroes.

So I reflect back to the question, "What made me the person I am today?" Of course I cannot count all of the little things in life that have added up to person I am. But my husband and daughters have truly given me their love and support, which gave me the confidence I needed to help other children. They have always supported all of my job decisions and endeavors! My daughters have given me the experience, inspiration and knowledge to inspire and work with other children. And in turn, the student population that I work with has made me realize the important things in life and define the true "challenges" in my life. I always try to do my best and to always try to help others be the best that they can be.

Being saved by these superheroes...
I became a *New Beautiful*.

MY UNEXPECTED BATTLE

I found a lump. It was a hard lump that I knew hadn't been there for very long. I was praying it was nothing but I had a nagging feeling it was something. I was 35, no family history of breast cancer, my kids were one, two, and three years old, and I had always taken good care of myself. I ate well, exercised, and was in pretty good shape. How could there be something really wrong with me? That was the scary thing: everything seemed to be going well. I was back at work after three consecutive maternity leaves. We were busy, but life was good… until I found the lump. One lump and life would never be the same.

I called the doctor a few days after I found it because I had a feeling -a fear- that it was definitely something. I couldn't look at my kids and my husband knowing it was there and there was nothing he could do about it. The doctor saw me right away. She examined me, and didn't think it was anything. She sent me for a few tests just in case. The "just in case" turned out to be a game changer.

The radiologist knew immediately it wasn't good. My head began to spin as she described what she saw and questioned me about my family history. I was sitting there, dressed for work, thinking I would go to work when my appointment was done, completely shocked by all that she was saying.

She wanted to biopsy it right away. Work was out of the question for that day, so I called my husband and tried as hard as I could to hold it together long enough to tell him what was happening. While I waited, things became a blur around me as I tried to wrap my head around what was happening. I was listening to the woman in the office talk about normal things to pass the time, and I just sat there trying not to cry, trying not to believe this was really happening. I kept thinking this couldn't be. Maybe she was wrong. She seemed so confident, "What if?" What if this *really* was happening?

The next two weeks were torture. We were pretty sure I had cancer, but had no idea how bad it was. And I had no idea what was ahead of us. My husband and I would sit at night, mainly quietly, and then one of would say, "Can you imagine I really have cancer?" The not knowing was horrible.

Finally the pathology report was in. I had Stage 2 breast cancer, estrogen and HER2neu positive. We had very big decisions to make and they needed to be made quickly. I wanted it out. I wanted it gone. The waiting was painful. My heart and spirit were broken. I, we, could not believe it. I was young and healthy. I didn't feel sick, and I was sick. Cancer became a part of our everyday discussions, our heads were reeling. We could not let on to the kids what was happening, but I was so sick with worry that I was a shadow of the person I had been before my diagnosis. It took everything I had to keep things normal for them. I wanted to crawl into bed and cry, but I couldn't. I had to go into fight mode, for myself, my kids, my husband and my family.

After meeting with doctors and discussing the prognosis, we scheduled surgery right away. I would need a bilateral mastectomy, eight rounds of chemo with four different drugs, and one year of Herceptin. I learned more about cancer than I ever wanted to know. I learned that the Herceptin that I would have for a year, along with the Tamoxifen I would be on for ten years, were the drugs that were available now to fight my specific cancer. The doctors told me about these life-saving drugs that have been developed to fight this horrible disease. When they say Making Strides Against Breast Cancer, they mean that woman can be treated on a case by case basis now, which allows so many more lives to be saved.

My husband came with me to every appointment, and we went into fight mode together. We just did the next thing the doctors told us, we couldn't think or plan very far ahead, we just showed up at whatever appointment was scheduled. We took in all of the information, talked about it, and walked around in a daze half of the time. We just got through it.

In what felt like one clean shot I lost my breasts, my hair, and my dignity. This wasn't the way it was supposed to be. My kids were babies, my marriage was young, and I was very sick. It was months before I could be home alone, months before I could drive or be alone with my kids- even for an hour. My children, my three blessings, were babies, and I couldn't take care of them. I spent my days in bed fighting, the little bit of energy I had each day went to them. I powered through and got out of bed for a little while every few hours so that life would seem a little normal to them. I had to explain to them why I couldn't lift them, hug them, or put them to bed after my surgery. As far as they knew I had "bad, bad, boo boos." I had to explain to them that I was going to lose my hair, and reassure them that everything would be ok soon. It was scary, every step of the way, and frustrating beyond words.

I would listen to them play, listen to life going on around me, and I could just be grateful for the help I had because I needed it. My children needed to be cared for, my husband needed to work, but we were lucky enough to have wonderful people around to help. They kept me going when I really didn't feel well, and pushed me to keep going even when I didn't want to. They made me laugh. Every night we had a dance party to Mickey Mouse Clubhouse, and them being there every day made a world of difference.

I remember my oldest child, who was three at the time, found a beach hat of mine that she really loved one day. She wore it all day, even though it was the dead of the winter, and after a few hours innocently said to me, "Mommy, I really like this hat, maybe someday when I have no hair. I can wear it." I smiled, fighting back tears, and then told her it was a lovely hat; and that she probably would always have hair, but she could certainly wear it whenever she wanted anyway. It was things like that that kept me in the moment, in mommy mode, and in survival mode. We would get through this.

My angel network was amazing. My family, friends, and colleagues gave me so much strength they could never know what their support meant to me. Every call, text, card, delivery, and visit was a much needed distraction, and a motivation to get out of cancer mode for a little while. I could do this because all of these people were behind me, they were pulling for me, and my kids and husband needed me. My family did whatever it took, my parents watched my kids, people did our food shopping, dropped off food; it was a godsend.

My husband took care of me like a trouper. He did whatever I needed without batting an eye. I was never embarrassed when he changed my bandages, helped me in and out of bed, or into the shower. He listened to me when I needed to break down, and walked slowly around the block pulling the three kids in the wagon on days I needed to get out. He sat through every appointment, and every treatment with me. Sometimes we talked, managed to make silly jokes to break the tension when we needed too, and sometimes we just sat quietly together in disbelief. While we patiently listened to the doctors and nurses, we were really just waiting to get back to our normal lives. When we left the chemo room we would go out for something to eat, or to the stores, so that I could process for a few minutes and get back on my feet before I went home to the kids.

I learned the true meaning of bravery and courage through all of this- feeling like you just can't do something for even one more minute, and somehow you do. It was difficult when people would look at me with a combination of sorrow and shock in their eyes, and not admit anything was wrong. I tried to just look at them with a smile on my face and give an "I'm alright" response because I had to fight and wanted to make them think I wasn't too bad off. I learned to appreciate people who could look past my peach fuzz covered head and didn't flinch, just acted like I looked normal, which we all knew I did not! I learned to appreciate the kindness of doctors and nurses, their honesty, and positive attitudes. The nurses were amazing; they took everything in stride, and showed hospitality and warmth in the treatment room which made a terrible situation a little bit better.

Eventually, after reconstruction, my body looked pretty normal, my hair grew back after chemo, and as my strength returned I was able to take back my old life. It took a long time to feel good after chemo, but with support and patience from the world around me, I did it, little by little. I appreciate life so much more now, when I think of all of the things I almost missed I am brought to tears. But I didn't miss them, and don't plan on missing anything else. My children hardly remember my worst days, which in itself are a blessing, and now I just focus on staying healthy. My family is great, I appreciate the little things every single day, and we are moving on. Life is good. Facing my unexpected battle head on, I became…..a *New Beautiful*.

PURA VIDA

I've recently discovered it's hard to define yourself, and I guess I've never really tried to do it before, or at least never attempted to write it down until I was asked by the most influential woman in my life. So when she asked me, the thoughts started to brew and then the writing began. Does one define themselves by a title? A daughter, sister, aunt, friend? Maybe it's by their status at a given moment? A girlfriend? A single woman in her 30s? I've decided that I'm best defined by my profession, a registered nurse. Not just any nurse, but an oncology certified nurse in the gynecological medical oncology department at a cancer hospital in a popular city.

I don't say that to sound like a hot shot, but I am proud that I have had the opportunity over the last nine years to work in such an amazing institution. In those nine years I have come to realize that it's not the fact that the institution is highly rated that makes it so amazing to work there, but it's the people that surround me every day. My colleagues, the patients, and the overwhelming amount of hope that surrounds those hallways has defined me as a person and influenced me to realize what is truly beautiful in this life of mine.

When self-reflecting, I think about these questions: Am I the type of nurse I am because of the daughter, sister, and friend that I have been raised to be? Or is now that I'm a cancer nurse defining the type of person I am in all my relationships and how I'm choosing to live my life? The answer is both. But I guess the answer to that really doesn't matter. What matters to me is that I am the best person I can be in both my personal and professional life. I am now able to see that my patients help make me the person I am today.

Because of my experience in this profession, I have tried to focus on living a "Pura Vida" life. So what does that mean? Its translation from Spanish to English is *pure life*. But more than that, its meaning is a theory of how life should be lived in the hearts and minds of Costa Ricans. I really connect my understanding of "pura vida" with the Pura Vida Bracelets definition; which to me means leading a life focusing on our blessings, taking the time to appreciate the good fortunes while never taking them for granted, slowing each day down long enough to celebrate and enjoy the gift of life, and making sure to live life to its fullest! It's keeping a positive attitude that every minute is worth living well.

I was lucky enough to take a trip in 2008 to Costa Rica with some of my amazing girlfriends where I first understood what that phrase truly means. It's hard to explain, but I left there a different person. A year later, I even branded myself with a *Pura Vida* tattoo. I challenge myself every day to live my life with the *pura vida* attitude, and hope to pass that along to the people who surround me, especially my patients.

It's hard to sit face to face with a woman who was just told she needs chemotherapy for the new diagnosis of cancer. I don't assume it will ever get any easier. But as hard as it is to witness, it could only be a hundred times harder to be the person receiving that information; they are forever changed. When a woman looks me in the eyes and cries, I immediately feel her strength, which then motivates me to be strong for her. Some people may question why I see strength in tears, but letting a stranger witness such emotion, such vulnerability: that is strength. When a patient I have known for years is told again that the cancer is back and more treatment is needed, I hold back tears. She takes my hand and says (with a stone face), "Ok teach me what I need to know." I admire that fighting strength.

This profession I have chosen is not an easy one. It has long hours, emotional and difficult situations, and has made me question my faith many times. So why would I choose such a thing? My patients of course! No matter how crazy or busy my day is, I still absolutely love going to work the next day. The women I have been lucky enough to meet on my career journey so far have forever changed my life, and continue to do it every day. I have been lucky enough to have patients that are appreciative for the care that I provide, and thank me over and over, but what I should really do is thank them. These women go from titles of wife, mother, and professional, and suddenly their lives come to a halting stop, getting turned upside down. They unwillingly replace their title to cancer patient. Not to say they are not the women they were before their diagnosis, but they are forever changed, along with their families. The strength and perseverance I see in these women is inexplicable. I don't necessarily just mean strength in the physical sense, but also emotionally and spiritually. I see women in their most vulnerable states, and I feel privileged to witness it and help support them; helping them through this time in their lives in group therapy and one on one. Daily, I am reminded that women are warriors! I would love to say because of my job I never complain about the unimportant things in life, but that simply isn't true and we're all guilty of doing it. But I can recognize when I'm complaining about insignificant troubles. An important lesson I've learned is to shut up and smile, while reminding myself how lucky I am.

All in all, I have a wonderful life. I may not have everything I hoped and wished for at 30 years old, but I do have a sister, parents, and amazing friends (that I consider family), who always give me unconditional support, surround me with laughter and adventure and truly accept me for who I am.

My definition of beautiful women has changed over the years, from skinny and flawless to dealing with a life-altering change and a fighting desire to live. I whole heartedly believe that all women are beautiful and that their beauty is not defined physically, but rather as a result of their struggles and defeats throughout their lives. I challenge the readers of this book to always look for a new beauty in life, and strive to live that life with a Pura Vida attitude while always having faith in themselves, faith in others, and faith in a higher power.

By constantly having faith... I've become a *New Beautiful*.

Running from What? Running to What?

For as long as I can remember food has been both a source of comfort and pain. Food is a connector, as it is in so many families. Watching others eat can have both a negative and positive effect on your life. What we are exposed to growing up shapes who we are.

My dad worked a lot so he didn't eat with us every night, however; he did like to cook with us. It must have been his Italian upbringing. Get closer with food. Food was a reward and a way to connect. It was a time where we talked and there was no judgment. He would tell me stories about how he used to cook with his mother and how connected he felt to her when he cooked with me. Food was just food then and it made me happy. I liked to eat and loved to dance! I was often told that if I didn't dance as much as I did, I would be "as big as a house." I vividly remember a ballet teacher once asking me if I had a cheeseburger for dinner. I suppose it showed on my leotard. And this started the foundation…

During college, I gained the "freshman 15" (pounds) but in my case a little more. I enjoyed life. I ate, drank, and didn't think twice about it. I auditioned for the dance team and became an alternate. I was pleased. The following year I auditioned again and I was cut. I was told I didn't take pride in my body. Translated…I was too fat. I didn't tell anyone until later on. I was embarrassed and I didn't want to get anyone in trouble. After all, I was the one who got fat. Instead of being on the dance team, I joined a sorority and they welcomed me for who I was. My size didn't matter. I was not a huge girl. I was actually average, 5 feet 4 in, 130 pounds. I became very involved in Greek life. It made me happy. I eventually became President, overseeing the sororities on campus. I was asked to join a group of peer mentors. It was a group that addressed the issue of eating disorders among sorority women. I learned a lot and later took up a minor in psychology focusing on eating disorders. We all joked that we knew so much about eating disorders that we could develop one. I developed one.

A year after I graduated college, life was good. I had a great boyfriend and I was happy. I began to take up running as a result of dating a Division 1 track and field grad. He inspired me to run; something that I always hated. I remember stopping soccer as a kid because I had to run and now I couldn't get enough of it. Everything was grand until… Mom got sick…I lost control. Control is a funny thing. You think that you have it when it is actually an illusion.

I didn't outwardly address her sickness. I internalized it. I got sick; sick with anorexia and exercise bulimia. Problem was, I didn't accept that I was sick. I didn't have a problem. I dealt with my mom's pain by suffering myself. I *couldn't* eat. I just felt sick. The pounds fell off but I wasn't trying to lose it I just couldn't eat. I told everyone I wanted to eat but I just *couldn't.* A bite here and a bite there was all I could do. I didn't think I had an eating disorder because I wanted to eat. After all that I had learned about the disease and tried to help others battle it, I developed it. In my eyes, I wasn't restricting my food, I just didn't feel good when I ate. In reality, I believed certain foods made me sicker so I was better off not eating them. That was the way I restricted.

Years later I can see that. I exercised because I was stressed and it made me feel better. A daily routine of two hours: in spin class or running on the treadmill, followed by a kickboxing class…this was normal for me. The eating and over-exercising went on for weeks which turned into months. I was scared. I didn't know what was wrong. I went for every test thinking there was something wrong. Every test came back negative. There was nothing physically wrong. The doctor finally said there was nothing wrong with my stomach; it was my head. It was something that I didn't want to hear nor admit. I thought to myself, "I know about eating disorders. I learned about them in college, I was peer mentor. I helped fellow sorority sisters work through them. I did <u>not</u> have one. I loved food. I wasn't anorexic."

But the 99 pounds on my 5ft 4in frame told a different story. People looked at me with worry. I saw it in their eyes because they never said a word. Everyone was afraid to talk to me and address my emaciated body.

My parents threatened me with hospitalization. I compromised and went to therapy. My therapist didn't address the eating alone. The focus was on me as a person. It wasn't food I was afraid of, it was me. He taught me how to fight and fight well. After a few months I was on my way. RECOVED NOT CURED.

Days and weeks passed. I began to regain weight even though I was happier at a thinner weight. I liked the way I felt thinner even though I know it wasn't healthy. People came up to me and told me I looked healthy. And by the way, don't ever tell a recovering anorexic they look healthy. To them it means fat. I went on knowing that it was because they cared. That school year came to a close and we had our annual end of the year brunch. My principal, at the time, put his arm around me and softly said, "Take care of yourself." It wasn't much but it meant a lot to me. I continue to battle the disease each and every day. I am reminded of what I have overcome in moments of weakness.

Throughout this time of struggle my Division 1 track star stayed by my side. He knew what eating disorders looked like but never made it a big deal. Sometimes I thought it was because he didn't care but I believe it was the best because we didn't draw more attention to it. We both knew it was there but we knew that talking and obsessing over it wouldn't make it any better.

Division 1 is a pilot. When we first started dating, he was getting his license while working at his family's tennis club. He worked very hard to attain his dream to fly. We were set up on a blind date and hit it off right away. He was an Ivy League graduate. He ran track. Smart and athletic. He was kind, funny, and loving. We dated for three years. Within those 3 years I was sick. He stayed with me. He was dedicated to me. We got engaged on a smelly boat dock. He wanted to do so much more but his nerves got the best of him. It didn't matter where he did it, we were getting married.

We got married and moved into our house. Division 1 finished his training and began flying medavac. I would pack him up and send him on his way. We wouldn't know how long he would be gone for. Sometimes it was days but usually it was weeks. We were newly married and he was gone most of the time. I told him if we could get through this time we could get through anything. Being married to a pilot is not easy; especially being married to one who does not fly for an airline but for a private charter company. He is on call all the time and only gets 3 days off a month. It is tough when he gets a call last minute and is gone for days.

After being married for two years, Division 1 and I started to talk about having kids. We were ready. We tried. Nothing happened. I was running more and restricting my food again. Now this time I knew I had a problem. I just kept running. It helped me relieve the stress of not being able to get pregnant. Then I decided I wanted to set a personal best. I trained and trained hard. I wanted to break 21 minutes for a 5k. I wanted it. I got it. What I didn't get was my period. It was months. I went to the doctor and he told me I had polycystic ovaries and my weight was too low as well. My body wasn't letting me get pregnant because I didn't have enough body fat to hold the pregnancy. As usual I disagreed. I thought I looked great. I was running the best I ever had. I was earning medals. I liked that feeling. My body was protecting me. The doctor tried different drugs to get my ovaries to produce eggs. I, of course, kept running.

My friends around me were getting pregnant and I was getting mad. Why them? I wanted to have a baby so badly and I couldn't. People told me to relax and it will happen. Try to relax when you are taking numerous pills a day and going to doctors appointments every other week. Instead, I started running. I decided to train for my first half marathon. I I had to run and it helped me alleviate stress. I ran with the girls each morning at 5 am and then went to work. It was how I started my day. The half marathon was the first weekend in May.

My doctor and I decided that I would take Clomid the Monday after the race. I told him that I would take some time off from running to see if it would work. It did. I became pregnant with my first son.

I was afraid of the weight gain. One of my running friends told me on a run that I wasn't eating for me but for the baby. This helped. I gained the average 25 pounds and exercised throughout the pregnancy. I had to stop running because I had some bleeding but continued with other exercises. The morning I gave birth I did my normal routine, went to the gym and then to work. My ankles were swollen but I figured it was because I was almost 9 months pregnant. I had a routine doctor's appointment that afternoon. He didn't like my blood pressure and weight gain so he sent me to the hospital. I was in labor. I didn't even know it. The baby was breech so I was into the delivery room for an emergency c-section. I told myself I couldn't be in labor, my mom was not in town. I wanted her there. There was no time. The doctor said he couldn't wait. Division 1 and my dad were by my side. I had a baby boy; 6 pounds 9 ounces 4 weeks early. He was born just before 36 weeks and considered premature so he had to go into NICU for observation. He was healthy and came home with me days later. I began nursing my baby boy. I heard that it was the best for the baby but I had an ulterior motive...weight loss. I read that it helped women lose the baby weight faster, I was in. It wasn't as easy as I thought. I was the only one who could feed him so all of the responsibility was on me. It was a lot of pressure.

I became resentful of my baby boy and my husband. He didn't get up twice a night to feed him. I was exhausted. I couldn't work out because of the c-section. I had no outlet.

I tried to remember that it was good for my baby boy. It was good for me too because the weight fell off. I was back to my jeans in no time.

Enter postpartum depression. I knew I wanted to be a mother. However; I felt like a bad mother because I didn't want my baby any more. The feelings consumed me. I couldn't leave my baby even though I needed a break. I cried and cried and cried. I began to eat because I was depressed. This was different for me. I didn't want to eat. I wanted to starve myself but I didn't have the power. I wanted to eat instead. I was filling the emptiness I felt with food. I would stand at the cabinet just eating because I was away from the baby. I hated what I was doing to myself but couldn't stop. I was powerless. I went to my OBGYN for my six week checkup and couldn't control my emotions. He put me on an antidepressant to take the edge off and I began therapy again. This time with a woman who specialized in postpartum depression. I didn't want to be there but knew I had to be. Therapy only works if you want it to. I went to my appointments and went through the motions.

After about two months I was done. If I kept going then I was going to "feel better" which to me meant I would gain weight. I wanted desperately to be back at my pre-baby weight, where I felt the best about myself even though others thought I was too thin. It just wasn't in the cards. I had a different life this time. I had a baby. As my baby boy grew my postpartum depression lessened. Some days it came back and the feelings of worthlessness were stronger than ever.

I had a support group, my friends and family. Division 1 would remind me that I was a good mother while holding me as I cried.

Day to day, I began to enjoy my baby even more. We laughed and cried together. He was my buddy. I wasn't alone when Division 1 went away. I didn't have to eat alone. I always had company. My baby boy became a mama's boy. Who could blame him? He was with me all the time. I loved but hated how attached he became. I felt loved but I wanted to have time alone too. Going to the gym was my only time alone. Once again, exercise was my *savior.*

I began taking my baby boy to the gym. I said that it would make me a better mom if I had time for me. It did. I felt better about myself. I couldn't over exercise even though I wanted to because I didn't want to leave my baby boy for too long. It was good for me.

When my son was a year and a half Division 1 and decided that we were going to have another baby. I went to the doctor and we started the process. We knew that we would have to take Clomid again. I took the first round in July nothing happened. I was devastated. We tried again. August we were pregnant.

Things were great until one night, I started bleeding. I had no idea what to do. I called my doctor and told me that he is not sure what it was from being that I was only 8 weeks pregnant. I got home and made the decision to go to the hospital. My parents, my saviors, came to my rescue. I went to the hospital and got looks of sadness. Bleeding in your first trimester typically equals miscarriage. At the hospital, I was sent for a sonogram, Division 1 and I tried to stay positive. I told Division 1 this is it. If we don't hear a heart beat it is over. As the sonogram tech looked at the monitor she reassured us that the baby was fine. Then she hesitated. Our hearts dropped. She took a minute and said she didn't just see one sac but two. We were having TWINS. It was an emotional rollercoaster. No one in the hospital could believe it; nor could my doctor who I saw the next day. Our lives would be changed forever.

As a result of my baby boy being early my doctor sent me to a high risk doctor. I was nervous about having twins but even more about the weight gain. I asked what the typical weight gain was. As usual I was concerned about my weight. The doctor told me 40-45pounds. I was amazed. I couldn't comprehend it. I was going to gain how much? I felt sick. He said, you can bring a horse to water but you can't make it drink. He said it was up to me as to what I wanted to do about weight gain. Instead of watching what I ate, I took advantage of being pregnant. I ate whatever I wanted. I devoured foods I normally would never touch. It was bagels for breakfast, chips and dip, and lots of dessert. It was my free pass. Foods that I had been restricting myself from eating were all fair game. I did not stop myself from eating. The crazy part was, I didn't gain exorbitant amounts of weight. I stopped myself when I was full because I knew that I could eat the foods again when I wanted. I wasn't binging because I never ate the food or didn't know when I would eat it again. In all this time I could barely work out. The babies wouldn't let me. I was put on bed rest.

The girl who could not sit still and wanted to work out all the time was not allowed to get off the couch. Ironic?! All I was allowed to do was lay, horizontal on the couch or in bed, go to the bathroom and take a shower. When I took showers I would wash myself as quick as possible because the babies were putting pressure on my cervix, which was shortening. I needed to keep the babies in. After I was done washing I would get onto all fours in the tub and let the warm water hit my back. It was the most peaceful part of my day. I would talk to myself and usually pray. I asked God to keep the babies in for a few more weeks. I wanted them to be strong and healthy when they came out.

Every day I would sit on the couch "watching" T.V., many times not even paying attention to it. I couldn't read or do puzzles, I just couldn't focus. I ate because I had to and I was bored. Being on bed rest helped me to not eat all the time. I couldn't get up. Toward the end I couldn't even sit at the dinner table because it was so uncomfortable. Bonus for me because then I wouldn't eat as much. The babies were growing strong so I was alright.

All this time that I was on bed rest, four and a half months, I still had my baby boy to take care of. I was able to drop him at our babysitter for a few hours a day. I couldn't pick him up or even sit on the floor with him. It was devastating. I felt like a horrible mother. I felt as though I was neglecting him but I had to take care of the two babies in my belly. One day I had told my high risk doctor about these feelings. He replied, don't worry baby boy will never remember it.

I did need help with my baby boy. I couldn't do it alone. I asked for help this time even though I hated to. It made me feel weak. I wanted to be strong and independent. I just didn't have the strength. I relied on my friends and family to help. Every day someone would be at my house by 4pm, when baby boy woke up from a nap. They would take care of him. He was getting more attention than he could imagine; but it wasn't from me. It killed me. I hated it. I became resentful of the twins. The twins that stopped me from working out. They stopped me from being the mom I wanted to be to my baby boy, and they stopped me from being intimate with my husband. Were they really worth it?

April 16th, I had a doctor's appointment. It was one of my weekly appointments. Division 1 had been on a trip for five days prior. I told him to drop me off, because I was no longer able to drive. The babies had taken yet another thing away from me - driving.

The nurse, who I got to know very well, put the straps across my belly and the twins were being monitored. My nurse came over periodically to check on me. I looked over and noticed a concerned look on her face. I asked, "What's the matter?" She replied, "Baby A is not moving like he should be." She sent me to the sonogram room to have a better look. She didn't feel comfortable with the report; she consulted the doctor. I was sent to the hospital for monitoring. When I got to the hospital my blood pressure was high and I was contracting. I was 35 weeks. I stayed in the hospital for hours, thankfully with Division 1 by my side. I dilated very quickly so once again I was rushed into the operating room for a c-section. Two OBGYNs, one doctor from NICU, 8 nurses, and an anesthesiologist rushed together to deliver my babies.

I kept those babies in for 35 weeks while only having 1 cm left of my cervix. I look back and am amazed I did that. Along the way I didn't think I would make it but I did. Baby A was born at 5lbs 5 oz. Baby B came second at 6 lbs 9oz. I wish I could say that they were born healthy with no complications, but the reality of it was they were in distress. They had swallowed their meconium. Baby A came out breathing on his own but Baby B didn't. Baby B needed CPR when he was taken out. He wasn't breathing.

The doctors and nurses took great care of my boys. Baby A and Baby B stayed in NICU for a week and a half being treated for pneumonia. I felt that this was my fault. I didn't keep them safe. My body just couldn't hold them anymore.

Watching those babies in NICU made me feel helpless. I couldn't do anything but stare at them. I couldn't hold them and barely could touch them. I imagined holding both babies when they were born, just like the pictures I saw, that didn't happen to me. I just watched monitors and prayed they would improve.

After two <u>long</u> days, the nurses asked me if I wanted to hold Baby B. I welled up with emotions. I wanted to but I felt that I would do more harm; however, I accepted their offer. I held Baby B for the first time and he improved. He knew his mommy. It was an amazing feeling. He didn't care what I looked liked or what I weighed or what I ate. He knew I was his mommy. He loved me already. The next day I was able to hold Baby A. I had the same result. I wanted to be with them at every moment. I was unsure as to what would happen next, when I left. Would they be okay? I didn't want to leave them. I felt like I put them in this position. The nurses told me I needed my rest too in order to be the mom they needed.

Nurses told me how wonderful I looked for just having twins. To me I was a mess. I was fat. I didn't want the weight on any more. I was done with it. I ate because I had to. I needed strength to take care of my kids. I wanted to starve myself to get the weight off but knew that it wouldn't help. I knew how to lose weight the right way but wanted a quick fix. I didn't give in. I was stronger than my illness. I had something else pushing me, my three sons.

Now, the twins are almost a year. I have lost all but 3 pounds of the 45 I gained. I am able to fit into my clothes, but now the number on the scale haunts me. I wonder if I will ever be able to lose those three pounds. My body is different. It is stronger. I look in the mirror and see my flaws like so many other women in society. I get lost in trying to obtain a number on a scale which is not a true measure of who I am. I am a woman who can take care of 3 kids when her husband travels for days or weeks at a time. I am a woman who summons the courage to ask for help even when she doesn't want to. I am a woman who has moments of weakness and sadness. I get anxious. I get depressed. I binge eat to heal an emotional hole. I want to starve myself to inflict pain from time to time but know it is the wrong thing to do.

I have a love hate relationship with food. I would kill for a stomach bug to lose 5 pounds. I am one who has an emotional attachment to a number on a scale. I am one who will judge her day on what the scale says. I cry. I have to fight to feel good about myself. I run to ease emotional pains and my workouts relieve anxiety. I love flipping tires and swinging a sledgehammer. I love the competition I have with fellow exercisers. I love a good long run with my girls. I love a run alone with my thoughts. I am a good teacher. I get caught up in what others think of me. I am loved by my three kids. I am loved by my husband. I am loved by my family. I am aware of who I am. I am not perfect; I have problems. I have friends and family who get me through them. I have friends who check in on me to make sure I am good. I have friends who will listen. I have friends who know exactly what to say. I have friends who tell me the truth. I am lucky to have such friends. I talk. I pray. I have been through stuff and continue to every day. I fight to be happy for my kids and husband.

I work hard each day to be my *New Beautiful*.

Two Suitcases

The world woke up to a dry, sunny day in March of 1992. Outside, the local sparrows chirped about a new spring. Inside, my eyes opened to the nightmare that had become my reality. Slowly, the large black suitcases came into focus revealing the pain that day would bring. Shirts, pants, and socks were piled high, ready to be flattened down and zippered shut. Life as I knew it would be wheeled away in those two suitcases. That day is burned into my memory as "moving-out" day. My husband of 17 years, and the father of our 3 and 6 year old sons, would leave us behind for a new life.

I first learned of his new life three months before that day. The news came to me as an arrow aimed straight at the heart. I clutched my chest as he admitted his secret. He had been with her more than six months. They met at work. Her husband was in jail for armed robbery. My husband set up a love nest for her, complete with furniture and electronics. I had been blind to it all.

Love is blind; betrayal is blinding.

There I was in the dark: teaching full time, playing with the boys after school, fixing their warm baths, cooking dinner every night, and reading bedtime stories to heavy-eyed toddlers who would fall asleep before their dad came home. His dinner was always waiting under a foil tent, but his hours grew later and later with each invented emergency that occurred at his job. f only he had the courage to tell me. I finally commented one night when he came home after 11:00 pm. "It's so late. I'm beginning to think you have a girlfriend." I said it sarcastically, like a joke. He looked down, holding his cowardly gaze to the floor. That's when I felt the arrow pierce.

The next three months would be a roller coaster. There was the moment he couldn't bear to leave me and the children. He promised to end the affair. My hope took flight. Then there was the night he ran down the back stairs to the kitchen in a panic. She was pregnant and might be losing the baby. He had to be with her. That revelation was too much to bear. My hope was extinguished.

On moving-out day, we told the boys after breakfast that life would be different…Dad would not be living in our house any longer. He would be living in a different house, but he would always see them and always love them. That psycho-babble didn't make any sense to 3 year old Peter, and 6 year old Jack. They hugged their dad and cried, not liking that idea one bit. I forced a smile for their sake, draining every ounce of my strength to fight back tears. Masking my fear, I assured them that everything would be OK. With the happiest voice I could muster I announced we would be going for haircuts, and a special lunch at Burger King. I didn't want the boys to see the suitcases carried to the car when their dad left.

With talk of kiddie meal prizes, we gathered in the foyer to get lightweight jackets on the boys. That would be the last time the four of us would stand as a family in the foyer of our home. I could hear my husband saying goodbye to our sons, but I couldn't process what was happening. I was numb. My stare moved up the turned staircase of that charming old house as the sun filtered through the delicate lace curtains on the diamond-paned windows. I just couldn't watch as Jack hugged his dad tightly and begged him not to move away. I took his small hand and opened the front door. I looked back at my husband one more time, my eyes pleading for a miracle, "You don't have to do this. We have built so much together. A loving family with two amazing sons. A beautiful home to hold our memories."

But the suitcases had the final word.

Suddenly, I was a single mom, holding my son Jack with one hand, and my son Peter with the other as we walked to the car. I strapped Peter into his car seat. A three years, he wasn't quite comprehending what was left behind. As I buckled Jack into his booster seat, he asked in a shaky, uncertain voice, "Mommy, if I was a good boy, would Daddy stay at our house?" My insides twisted with worry for this innocent 6 year old boy - a fine, well-behaved boy- thinking he hadn't been good enough to earn his dad's love. I tenderly kissed Jack on the forehead, reassuring him that his dad would always love him.

The children are the innocent victims.

The boys sat in their regular chairs at the barber shop, each draped in a black plastic cape. But there was nothing regular about that moment. I listened to the buzz of the electric trimmer as the barber created clean lines along the nape of their necks and around their ears. But all I could hear was the racket of confusion in my brain. How could I possibly take care of two boys alone? My vision of the future was dark, and I felt terrified.

After lunch we stopped at our friend Linda's house. Linda was the first person I had called in January, when I learned of my husband's affair. As soon as he left for work that next morning, I frantically dialed Linda's phone number. Voice shaking, I couldn't find words to explain the disgusting details. Within minutes, she was at the front door. My eyes were puffed with grief and exhaustion. No sleep had come to ease my anguish. Linda looked worried. She asked if my husband put his hands on me. I shook my head. "No, it was a different assault. It was an assault on our marriage and our children."

As Peter flew around us in his batman pajamas, I told Linda the tale of betrayal. Her shock and disbelief mirrored the response of all who would soon hear the news. No one believed this could happen to the couple who seemed so happy, the couple who enjoyed professional careers, the couple blessed with two healthy sons, and so many reasons to be grateful. No one could believe it was true.

It felt surreal to me, too. But it was real.

I knew the suitcases would have already been gone when I stopped at Linda's house on moving-out day, but I dreaded going home. Her children, Alice and Sam, were excited to see Jack and Peter, and within minutes the gang had disappeared to the playroom in the basement. Linda and I had a cup of tea at the kitchen table. I showed her a letter I composed to send to the other woman- the home wrecker. In the letter I poured my heart out as a wife and mother, hoping to appeal to her social conscience. Didn't she realize she was breaking up a happy home, with two very young boys who needed their dad? Linda and I analyzed every sentence in the letter. I prayed it would change the course of the storm destroying my marriage.

But nothing would change the path of destruction. Not everyone has a social conscience.

As the sun went down, it was time to go home to face our new reality. My husband would not be there, and he would not be coming home. Nausea crept up my throat as we got ready to leave Linda's house. Jack asked if Alice could come home with us for a sleepover. Of all nights for a sleepover. Linda and I agreed, both of us sensing why Jack had asked. Without a word spoken, we both understood that a 6 year old boy was preparing for the pain waiting for him in that big house abandoned by his dad.

And so it was...

Like a funeral procession we moved toward the front door. I was carrying Peter in my arms since he had dozed in the car. Jack and Alice led the way carrying pillows and pajamas for the sleepover. Not one light was there to guide us. We had left so early in the day we didn't think to leave to porch lamps lit. Halfway into the dark entry, we were brushed by an empty chill…ghosts of future memories never to happen in that house. Jack let out a loud wail, "Oh, no! My dad doesn't live here anymore." Alice stepped closer to him as he leaned his head on her shoulder and sobbed.

I will always remember that moment. Alice was the first of many who would step up close with a shoulder to lean on for comfort, hope, and support. There would be friends, neighbors, colleagues, teachers, brothers, sisters, cousins, nieces, nephews, and a dear father who would step up close and provide a shoulder to lean on as we journeyed from breakdowns to breakthroughs. We made it to the other side. With a circle of love and support around us, we learned that on the other side of the pain was a *New Beautiful*.

The Love that Surrounds Me Has Changed My Life

I lost my mother when she was a young 50 years old. I still think about her often and it has been 30 years since her passing. I remember her every birthday, every anniversary, and honestly, on a daily basis. Each time I see a red cardinal, I think of her. It's almost like she is the red cardinal flying in to check on me or maybe watch over me. When other people tell stories of their parents, I always immediately make the personal connection to my mother because she is so close to my heart and thoughts. The reason I still always think about her is because we were so close. I loved her with all my heart. And luckily, I could say all the same things about my father. He passed away young as well. I loved him dearly and was very close to him also.

So my daughters were young when I lost my mom. They were 14 months old and 3 ½. Being a mother of two young children, when I lost my mom, was so hard because there was such a big void of a "Nana" in our lives. I would have loved for her to be here to watch my children grow up, even just to hold them in her arms.

You go your whole life looking up to your mom and she looks down on you. And then you realize you never stop doing that…I feel like she is always looking down from heaven.

Being a mother is a job, but truly to me it is more of an honor. But that doesn't mean there were never any challenges to that. When my girls were growing up I wished I could take away all the hurt and pain that ever crossed their paths. I would always want to take the pain away and give it to me instead. My older daughter was diagnosed with a chronic disease at a young age. There was so many days of fevers and pain. I wish I could have taken it away. Anytime another child hurt my children emotionally, it broke my heart. But then again, you have to let them grow up and handle things on their own. I needed to be a support, I couldn't do it all for them. This is a big challenge as a mom, but I wanted to raise independent children as well.

I feel like it is so important to make your feelings explicit to your children. I always tried to be as fair as I could with both of them. I would always say, "I don't even love one of you one grain of sand more." My husband and I have always worked as team. Together we planned family trips, day trips to the beach, dinner outings, traveled on soccer trips, and socialized with family and friends throughout our children's lives. There was happiness, laughter, and love.

And in a blink of an eye, they grew up. Now, they are successful in their careers. My husband and I don't like to take credit for it when we are told you did a great job raising your girls. We say, "They are where they are today because of all <u>their</u> hard work." And watching them through the years made me feel just so proud and honored that I could say, "These are my girls."

I have always loved the quote, "A daughter is someone to hold in your arms when she's small and to hold in your heart when she's grown."

Another generation of our family was started four years ago. My daughters called my mother "Nana" and now being a grandmother of two, I feel honored to carry on the name "Nana" but as my four year old grandson likes to call me "Nana Jr." I feel like I have taken over for my mother, and I hope each day to make her proud as she looks down from heaven.

I can honestly say that being a grandmother has come so naturally for me. I worship the ground that my grandchildren walk on. I love them with all my heart. I am lucky enough to spend time with them almost daily.

Love has surrounded me my entire life. I adore my husband and love him to death. I am not a woman who worries about fancy clothes or fancy jewelry, but for me it has been the people around me that define my happiness. I have so much love in my heart for my family. And so motherhood made me...a *New Beautiful.*

"Reza," Pray

It's 8:00 AM and we're rushing from home to get to school. It's a short drive to their elementary school. Everyone is quiet in the car. My son Joseph is usually chatting with me, but he is quiet and his sister is in deep thought. I'm flipping through the radio stations when he asks, "Mom, who gets cancer more, boys or girls? Is that what you have? Cancer?" His questions took my breath away. I replied "You have nothing to worry about; one in a million has what I have. There is no chance that you'll get this, and you are perfectly healthy." "So I won't get all of those dots that you get mommy?" "Nope I promise," I said reassuringly. Not convinced, he asked, "Is it contagious?" "No honey, the dots come and go and they sometimes make me feel tired. That's why some mornings it's hard for me to get up and get going." We're finally at school and the conversation has moved on to an argument between him and my daughter over why her school bag is touching his. For the moment he was satisfied with my answers. With that, I take a deep breath and move on to the next part of my day, work.

All of what Joseph said was true; it's just so surprising to me how he put everything together, that there is something going on with my health. It's a form of cutaneous lymphoma. I thought because I never let having this condition interrupt my routine or everyday life, that my children wouldn't notice or know. Well, as they continue to teach me, they know more than we think. Looking back, I guess I did as well when I was a child.

My parents sent us to Catholic school. My father worked at a famous art museum and we lived in a small two room apartment in Queens, NY. The building where we lived stood out amongst the others in the neighborhood. It was clear from the chipping paint and the faint smell of urine in the hallways, that it needed some care to say the least. My sister and I shared a room and my parents slept on a couch in the living room/ kitchen/dining room, the all in one room as I thought of it. Although as a family we did not have as much in comparison to some of my childhood friends, I never felt that I was missing anything. Somehow I felt that we lived a rich life.

When I think of my mother in my early childhood, I remember her as often being "sick," and needing to be hospitalized once in a while. When she was hospitalized, I wasn't allowed to visit her and missed her terribly. Upon her return each time, I would make her a welcome home sign and bake a cake. Sometimes she seemed very quiet and not herself, almost in a catatonic state. At which point I thought that maybe she was still sick and that I just needed to give her more time. Other times she almost seemed like a different person. She wore more make up and more jewelry than usual, and spoke in a different way. Her mannerisms were completely different. I knew that something was not right with her, but I didn't question any of what was going on. This was just the way things were in our lives I guess, our norm.

My childhood was filled with unpredictability, fluctuating with my mother's mood swings. When I was younger it seemed as though no one could help her. We never knew what to expect from her on a day to day basis. However, the one constant was the love that she gave. Despite her day to day battle with getting up in the mornings and simply getting dressed, she made sure that my older sister and I had everything that we needed. In the Hispanic culture and particularly my family, you did not share what happens within your family with others. No one knew what our day-to-day struggles were.

Faith was something that was very important to my family, and what I believe has guided us through our most difficult times. We went to church every Sunday, sometimes the Spanish mass (which always took longer). My mother went every day after she dropped us off at school. There was always holy water under our beds for protection, and a shrine of saints lit with candles and gifts for each of the saints, based on what each of them is known for liking. My mother also made sure that we had a picture framed of the guardian angel above our beds. Whenever we encountered difficult times, my mother always said in Spanish, "Reza (Pray)." I always felt that everything would be better after we prayed, or at least it seemed that way.

When I was in 8th grade, my mother was able to maintain a job working as a security guard at the same art museum as my father. We were able to move to a safer home, and things were starting to seem better. My mother was getting sick less often, and things were starting to feel more stable.

In my sophomore year of high school, my sister who is six years older than me went to study abroad in England. This was the first time we were ever apart and I felt really lost at home without her. It was during this time that my mother went through a period where she was really "sick" and had severe manic/hyper episodes. I was older and very aware that there was something really wrong with her. No matter which doctors she saw or how many different medications she was on, she wasn't getting better. Her changes in personality and bouts of depression were increasing now with severity and intensity. There was no stability in her behavior. Sometimes she would leave the house for hours and we had no idea where she was.

When she was manic, religion played a major role. There is one particular episode that I remember very well. We were looking for her in the neighborhood and couldn't find her. We walked to a shopping center not too far from our house. I saw a group of girls that I recognized from my high school leaving a clothing store that I really liked. I was praying that my mother wouldn't be found there. My prayers would not be answered this time. There was a bus at a stop and police officers were standing on the steps entering the bus. My father and I slowly approached the bus. I had this overwhelming, sinking feeling that I would find my mother there. The officers were addressing someone on the bus in a surprisingly very gentle tone. They were trying to get this person off the bus. As we stood behind the officers a very familiar voice sounded from on the bus. I spoke to my mom loud enough so that she could hear me. When she heard my voice, she willingly exited the bus. The officers reported that she had been preaching on a public bus. You see she believed that she was one of Jesus' disciples and that she was sent to spread the word of God. I kept glancing back at the group of girls from my school, hoping they didn't notice me. We ensured the officers that we would take it from there, but they insisted that she be taken to the hospital. She was taken away right before my eyes.

At this point she hadn't been diagnosed appropriately and the doctors did not have any answers for us. She had been on many different medications, none of which worked. My father didn't know what his next plan was; before that, he always seemed to have a plan to make things better. Her psychiatrist felt that it was time to admit her to a psychiatric facility. My father turned to me teary eyed and said "I don't know what to do. What should we do?" I was fifteen years old. With tears streaming down my face I said let's see how else they can help her. Then I prayed.

A new doctor, a young resident, joined her team of doctors at the hospital. After meeting with my mother and us, he immediately diagnosed her correctly with manic depression (now referred to as bipolar disorder), and gave her lithium. His diagnosis saved her and our family. Although she was stable most times, she still had episodes. Her psychiatrist was always there for us, and still is 27 years later.

We never lost our faith that she would be better. Our religion is something she instilled in us as children and what we have always held on to. It was through her strength and determination to get better that we pulled through the most difficult times.

My mother continues to amaze me with her humility. She is somehow able to find laughter in all that she went through. We can retell stories of her episodes and while some of them are very upsetting, we can find the humor in it all. There was never any doubt in our minds that things would be okay, we had our faith and love.

It's two weeks later after our discussion in the car. It's a Monday morning and my husband kisses me on my forehead to gently wake me up before he leaves. He asks me if I'm able to get up and if there is anything I need before he leaves for work. This isn't a good morning for me and he knows this. Joseph bounces in my room and reminds me that it's 7 AM and that we need to leave soon. I reassure him that I'm ready to get up, and that it's just a little hard for me today. After getting ready, I come downstairs to find that they are both dressed and that Joseph has made the lunches for him and his sister Louise. I tearfully hugged them both. How was I so blessed with such a beautiful family that is filled with love and thoughtfulness?

My family is where I draw my strength from now. Because what I have is so rare, there isn't much research on it. As I'm writing this I haven't had a lesion in over a week. This is the longest I've gone without one in about 2 and a half years. I know that this may change again at any moment, but I truly believe that this is because of the daily prayers that my mother says for me. And maybe even because of the picture that she has of me next to one of her saints. Either way, I have faith in that everything will be okay.

There are milestones in your life that define who you are and will become. I know that I was naturally more independent than most children, and now as an adult I can appreciate that my experiences growing up have given me strength to persevere through any of life's challenges or obstacles that I may face. For this I have my mother and my faith to thank…and I became a *New Beautiful*.

Everything Happens
for a Reason

The first sign I ever bought to hang in my house said "The Most Important Things in Life Aren't Things." I love signs. I have always loved quotes and inspirations. They make me feel good, feel positive and remember to always look for the messages in life that will help guide me... or make me laugh (both equally important!). I never thought they would mean so much to me and I would end up collecting so many!

I thought I had it all... the husband, the baby, the job, the house, etc. I really thought I was happy. It wasn't an easy beginning when I got married but I thought I had made it through the tough times. Here's how it all started. After I received my undergraduate and graduate degrees, I started my career as a preschool special education teacher in a public school in a suburb of Northern Virginia. I was excited. It was my beginning. I felt enthusiastic and was enjoying my single life hanging out with friends on weekends and working all week in my new job. Shortly after I began my second year of teaching…9/11 rocked my world. I remember going into the faculty room to watch the news and watching the towers go down. I was speechless. I couldn't believe it. I felt so far away from home. At the same time, I was so close to the Pentagon and we were on alert for planes flying over our school, as our school was minutes from Republic Airport. It was that day that I start missing my family in NY. I started to worry about what would happen if something happened to one of them. Unfortunately, in the years I was away at college my parents divorced, something I never saw coming. I had avoided dealing with it by staying away from where I grew up in NY. Now, I worried about each of them being alone.

About a month after 9/11, another significant tragic event changed my life. It was around noon. My students had left for the day. As I was walking toward the office to check my mail I passed the computer lab. One of our male 5th grade teachers came running out saying that our technology teacher had passed out. He was shuffling his 5th graders out of the room as the office was alerted to call 911. I ran into the computer lab and there she was on the floor. She was unconscious, blue… lifeless. I immediately started checking her airways for breathing not knowing what had happened… was it a stroke, had she just hit her head, was it a heart attack? I had prepared for this day that I never thought would actually happen, the day I had to utilize my CPR training. Just as I was about to begin, our school nurse ran in to help. One, one thousand, two, one thousand…

I just started thinking about what you see in the movies. For thirteen minutes I did chest compressions while our school nurse did mouth to mouth. It took that long for the ambulance to arrive. Our school was situated in a more remote area and it felt like an eternity for that ambulance to arrive. By the time they arrived she had regained her color. The crew hooked her up and before I knew it she was in an ambulance on the way to the hospital. I was numb. I had never been so close to death in my life. It scared me.

I'll never forget being in my car on my way home from a home visit later that day. It was my school nurse, she told me to pull over. She then proceeded to tell me that the hospital called and said we saved her life. She had a heart attack. Although I was supposed to feel more like a hero, I felt sad… I knew it wasn't going to be that easy. I was there and remembered how she looked lifeless on the floor. In the next few days we found out that she had lost too much oxygen before we arrived to perform CPR. She was brain dead and they were going to make the difficult decision to remove her from life support. She died. I was heartbroken. She was an inspiring woman full of life and energy and only in her late fifties. I went to her memorial and sat quietly in the corner. I knew that day I needed to move back home to NY to be close to my family.

A week or two later I decided to make a trip home to let my family know I wanted to permanently move home the following summer. This was a huge decision for me, but one I needed to make. That weekend while visiting home, I met my husband. I knew of him practically my whole life. He went to school with my older brother and grew up around the block from me. In fact, when I was younger I could see him from my bedroom window playing with his brothers in his driveway. One of my best friends was his cousin, who lived next door to him. I dated his brother's good friend for a brief time when we were in high school. So many connections we had. I was so ready to be in love and get married. It felt like the perfect love story I'd always dreamed about. We dated long distance for the remainder of my school year before I moved home. Everything was perfect until my brother began expressing his feelings about my new boyfriend. He did not want me to marry him and he would do anything to stop it, even get my parents on board. I was so sad… here this was supposed to be the happiest time in my life and my entire family was up against me. It felt so unfair. We even went into family counseling over it. One day I decided to go to the bookstore to find a book that would help me through this difficult time. I picked up the Four Agreements by Miguel Ruiz (a must read!). I read it in one day. I'll never forget the feeling I had after reading that book… a weight had been lifted. I knew I was going to stand by my decision and not look back. My family could choose to support me or not, but I was going to get married to the man I loved.

My brother didn't attend my rehearsal dinner and almost didn't show up to my wedding. Our relationship definitely suffered during those times but eventually shortly after the birth of my daughter, he started coming around. I was happy and he saw it. That's when it happened. My world was rocked to the core. My daughter was about a year old and I was ready to try for baby #2. My husband told me he wasn't happy. I suggested starting counseling. I too was feeling overwhelmed and disconnected at times (wasn't that normal for a young couple who just had a baby?) and thought this could be great for us. It could make our marriage even stronger. Counseling didn't go that well. He just wasn't putting the effort in, it felt one sided. Then, on the day before my birthday, I discovered something that turned into the beginning of the end. I was on the phone with a friend from work talking about what was going on in my marriage and she said, "Do you think he could be cheating on you?" I immediately responded "No way!" If I knew anything at that point, he may have been a lot of things, or lacked in certain areas… but loyalty was his strong point, never would he do that to me! After I hung up the phone, I checked our phone bill. This is something I had never done before, never even thought to do. What I found made me feel like I just got punched in the stomach.

The year that followed was pure misery. I was depressed, lost weight, became a professional private investigator (lol!), lost my husband and the dream of a happy family with siblings for my daughter. It was a co-worker he had apparently been having an affair with for some time. I had no idea. In fact, I kissed that very girl hello a week prior in an attempt to try harder to make connections with his friends and co-workers to show my support (something he told me he needed me to do for him while we were in therapy).

I used to write letters to her to help me with my anger. I never sent them, but it did help to get my feelings out. I hated her. I hated her more than I hated anyone in my life… including my husband, who was a close second. I knew my anger was misdirected, but I didn't care. Going through a divorce was devastating and painful. The hardest thing I ever had to do in my life. I didn't know who I was. I went temporarily crazy and became obsessed with proving the truth. When someone you trusted continually lies to you and tells you that you are the crazy one… you become an empty soul as you struggle with the truth and grasping the concept that a human being you loved can do something so hurtful to you. Therapy helped. I had so much support from family and friends. I bought a lot of signs! Quotes, inspirations, and music helped me through. I still hear certain songs and flashback to different moments throughout the process. Each day got a little better, good days turned into weeks then months.

I dated. I dated a lot! I loved online dating. I know it's not for everyone, but I committed to it. I met a few great guys and had some great relationships, but never met the one. Things were going really well though. I was feeling normal again. Then my mom got sick.

Stage 4-breast cancer with metastasis in her bones was the final diagnosis. It was surreal. She was so sick. My flight or fight mode took over and I became her primary caregiver. I took over on an adrenaline rush. We made a makeshift bedroom in my dining room. I ran out and bought binders and dividers to keep track of all her paperwork and medications. Her doctor at one point commented how she had never met anyone so organized and on top of someone's care before like I was. Here I was a single mom trying to take care of my daughter and my mom. Why me? It wasn't fair! I had just overcome the failure of my marriage and now I am faced with another inevitable devastating loss in my life. My mom fought hard and got back on her feet in a few months. She moved back home and did really well for a while but eventually the cancer was rampant in her body.

I always felt grateful that I was prepared. I did and said everything I needed to so that my mom knew I loved her and would do anything for her. Part of my soul died the day I had to take the ambulance ride from the hospital to hospice because there was nothing left to do. The day she died, I was alone with her in her room holding her hand. We had stood by her bedside every day for two weeks. I secretly and selfishly prayed that when the moment came it would be just her and me… and it was. It was actually a very special day. We had all decided to let the kids in the family come to the hospice center to visit. A decision I struggled with, as my daughter was only five years old. It was actually beautiful though. My two nieces, my young cousin who was like a grandson to my mother, and my daughter sat quietly around her bed drawing pictures and hanging them up around the room for "Nonnie." As the day was winding up I needed to drive my daughter home to her father as I was going to stay for the rest of the night by my mom's side as we had done for the past couple of weeks. I felt no sense of urgency as my mother had not exhibited any changes and was not showing any signs that today was going to be any different. When I returned, everyone (my dad, my brother and sister-in-law, aunts, uncles, etc.) was sitting in the sunroom next to her room. It was the first time in days that she was alone. My father told me quietly that everyone left to see if maybe she wanted to be alone.

The workers at the hospice center told us that people die in the way they want to... sometimes alone, sometimes waiting for everyone they love and sometimes with someone special. We all thought maybe my mom was holding on until she could be alone. I decided to step in the room with my mom as I was looking forward to a quiet moment to be alone with her. I sat quietly holding her hand. That's when it happened. She took her last breath. As I wept, I felt an overwhelming comfort that my mother just gave me the biggest gift she could at that point. I can never explain how I felt at that moment.

I was very lucky. My parents were amazing role models. Although they divorced when I was in college, they turned out to be best friends. It was not an easy process in the beginning for them, but slowly my brother and I and the concept of family drew them close again. People always asked us if we thought they would marry again and my answer was always "No way!" They were so different, yet I knew they loved each other. Neither really had any other relationships to speak of since they divorced. They spent every holiday together, every birthday and spoke practically every day. I will never forget one particular day my father was coming over to visit when my mom was living with me. At this point she was pretty sick, her bed now at the bottom of my stairs in my living room so I could hear her if she called and needed me. She was sitting on her bed, bald and so pale, putting makeup on her face because my dad was coming over and she wanted to look pretty. It was the first time I saw my mom put make-up on in a while. This was a prior daily ritual of which she would never leave the house without completing. My heart breaks every time I think about that moment… bittersweet.

So… does everything happen for a reason? I'm not sure I can find the reason why my mom had to suffer and I had to lose her at such a young age (she was only 60). But, I can find the solace that comes from tragedy. Knowing that I said and did everything I could for my mom when she needed it most, knowing that through her loss I learned to appreciate everything she did for me and how all of who I am is because of her. I feel so spiritually connected to her and believe in the signs that she gives me that she is around me all the time. No one can take those things away from me. I feel so grateful to have been her daughter and proud of all she had overcome in her life.

When I look back at my divorce, I can say that everything happens for a reason. My daughter is that reason. She was not an easy child to raise…"strong willed" is an understatement! But, she is my heart. She is everything to me and I am so proud of who she is turning into. I have always stayed positive. I cried when I needed to but faked a smile too until one day it felt real again. A little over two years ago my dream came true. You see, I always had this dream that my life would turn out like one of those love stories you see in the movies. I was disappointed the first time around, but never gave up on getting it right the second time! I knew it probably wasn't rational but I still wanted it. I did constantly question whether getting the life I always wanted was possible, but I never gave up. Everything I have gone through made me stronger.

You see, I always tried to remember… good things happened to good people. I always considered myself a good person. I always think of others before myself… almost to a fault. I was just waiting for my "good thing." My good thing turned into a great thing. His name is Jon and he truly is my Prince Charming. I wasn't so convinced the first few dates. I fact, I almost messed it up in a big way in the very beginning, but he took a chance on me. The day I knew he was the "one," was when we went on a date for the first time with our daughters. It was very early on and he really wanted us to see each other. We both had our kids that weekend and it happened to be his birthday. Jon casually mentioned maybe it would be a nice idea to "run into" each other at the bowling alley, as friends. I had no problem with it and thought it would be nice. Within a few minutes at the bowling alley one of his girls sat on his lap and whispered something to him. As he blushed, I of course asked what she said. He told me she said "Hey Daddy, if you marry her, one day we could be a family." Wow, I thought. These girls are very new to the life of divorced parents (Jon was only separated from his wife for a year or so) and that was an interesting comment. A short while later his other daughter stated out loud, "It feels like we are a family." I'm thinking "Holy cow... this is getting really interesting!" We immediately clicked as a family that day. It was unexplainable. Things were going so well that we decide to go out for ice cream afterwards. Jon and I sat in the chairs of the empty ice cream shop and watched the girls prancing around and laughing. They were 6, 7, and 8 years old at the time. I remember just feeling warm and fuzzy... smiling at Jon and feeling over the moon. As we left and said goodbye one of the girls mentioned how comfortable we were around each other. It was like they knew something we didn't yet. Then we said our goodbyes for the day and my daughter and I headed into the car. As soon as the car door shut my daughter said, "Mommy, I feel funny calling him Jon." I replied, "Why? That's his name." She told me "Because I want to call him my step dad." My stomach dropped... was this really it?

Yes... it was and still is. My story didn't end. It just goes on happily ever after. Everything does happen for a reason. You just have to be patient and wait to find out why. I promise, if you stay positive and use all the experiences in your life to reflect on how to be a better person and make the best decisions you can you will see that every single thing that happens in your life will lead to you where you want to be. Everything happens for a reason.

PS: If I were to write a letter today to that "other woman" who changed my life. It would look like this:

Dear Sarah,

Thank you. I had no idea that what you did to my family would end up being the best thing to ever happen to me. I have a great relationship with my ex-husband, who happens to be an amazing dad to my daughter. My daughter was so young when this happened (she was only a year and a half old) that she knows no other life, and I am so grateful for that. She is so well adjusted and loves her mom and dad so unconditionally and equally, that it makes me feel proud. The position you put me in forced me to realize, I too was not happy and deserved so much more than I was getting. I learned so much about myself and I healed. I have always been able to reflect and that helped me so much.

I did so many new things to help myself recover from the heartache... I learned to be me again. I flew to Australia by myself, went skydiving, and starting running 5Ks again... to name a few! Most importantly, you gave me a second chance. My second chance's name is Jon and he is truly my partner and soul mate. I would have never had the opportunity to find him had I not been forced into a situation I didn't ask for or want back then. I could always put my head down on my pillow at night and sleep well knowing I did everything I could to save my marriage. But it takes two... and it couldn't be done alone. Thank you for giving me this chance in life. I can now say for the first time as I am writing this... I forgive you. I hope you find the happiness I did. Always remember... everything happens for a reason and I hope one day you find your "New Beautiful" just like I have.

Sincerely,
Beth

TEXT MESSAGES

Simple words and communication can be relationship changing. My husband (but at this time, new boyfriend) worked nights and I worked days. When we actually had time together, I wanted to talk more and he is a man of simple words. I am the jabber jaw. I love to talk. I talk all the time…probably too much sometimes. We had busy schedules. So when we actually got to eat dinner or a meal together, I wanted to reflect on the day with him. I wanted to hear about his day. How was work? What did you do? Who aggravated you? Who supported you? But he liked the television on, the I-pad out, and the I-phone group texts, sports updates, and a Facebook newsfeed rolling.

At a point of almost frustration, I said, "Turn off the technology and talk!" My boyfriend (husband now) said, "We talk all day. What do you mean?" At that very moment I stopped and thought, oh yeah, we do. I realized that compromise is important. And what is really important in a relationship is understanding from your partner's perspective. So I started saving my text messages and those little comments really added up to heartfelt, funny, and sometimes eye opening moments. I realized and loved that his little messages may not be the "fairy tale, romantic mush," but in his way, he was expressing himself and taking small moments throughout the day to write, that meant he was thinking about me all day. And to me, that was quite romantic! After I *read* his texts, our relationship became…a *New Beautiful.*

Here are some of the texts:

-I'm up now baby call me when you can

-Good morning sunshine

-U were a fabulous date

-Nope we will watch it together

-I'll see you after school tonight and give u a great big hug and kiss

-Miss ya babe

-U go girl

-Whatever u wanna do hun….but I am broke till Friday so whatever u wanna do has to be free

-Ok I'll be at the gym till 330 so just come here when u can

-Ok babe….miss you

-Morning my sweet…have a great day and I can't wait to see u later

-Sweet dreams babe…call me when u get up…xoxo

-I don't know what to write so I just want u to know I am thinking bout u

-Muah baby!!! Can't wait to see u later…have a great day…

-Sweet dreams princess

-U fit perfectly

-I also have your necklace…and I think ur amazing…I miss you

-Hope ur having fun…give your sister a big birthday slap on the ass for me ;0

-Baby ill hangout with u all weekend during the day if u want

-Muah baby!!! Can't wait to see u later…have a great day…

-U r the best….muah

-Morning sweetness

-Thank u again for everything

-Take a sick day and hang out with me

-Miss u babe…wish u were with me

-Oh please knucklehead I told u that u r never a bother

-Sure I would love to wake to ur voice…

-Me dranky drank too much with lil sleepy sleep

-I miss u…I don't like three days of no you

-Definitely…u better see me

-I'm ok but gave 80 as a tip so I'm broke for Thursday night…u were an awesome hit…Michelle and Ray and u were great together

-You are my great one I am all yours…will be forever and forever

- Night baby…thank u for being awesome

- Good morning my sweet…

- Call me when u r free babe…im up

- Good morning munchkin

- Morning sweet thang ;)
- Yes but I feel bad im not with u today
- Hi bebe im home and I wish u were here
- I wanted to come back to u
- Take off and stay with me
- Do not go to work
- So take a day off and stay with me…call now
- I hope my mom is ok…I love you
- I love you…that's all I have to say
- You look sexy every night
- Oh? That's all u got? LOL
- U r amazing baby…miss u and can't wait to see you later…xoxo
- Did u make it home?
- Hey Sweet heart call me whenever ur free
- I'm ok baby…missed u today
- Hi my love…thinking of u
- Thank u so much for taking me to my parents…I love you…xoxo
- I always want u
- Baby I don't like when u r upset now it's on my mind
- U need me I'm always here for u. just speak up. I hope I didn't offend u in anyway
- I'm off til Sunday night…it's party time woo hoo
- I love you baby…xoxo

FAITH

I was so thrilled when the idea of writing a chapter for this book was presented to me. People I know will be surprised, rightfully so, by my chapter. Perhaps not so much about the struggle itself, but the details and the length of time it endured. I have never shared any of the information with anyone, except of course those who were on a need to know basis. So, why now? Sympathy? Certainly not. Millions of people have had similar experiences. I pray for them. First, it was a personal issue and I wasn't really ready to share it with others, whereas now I feel like it might help someone. Equally as important, I didn't want to upset anyone with the details and now there is nothing left to be upset about! There were other reasons as well, but I am glad I never shared my story; it adds an element of suspense to this chapter, no?

I suppose beginning with a warning would be best. This chapter will contain some "TMI" so if you are someone who easily becomes uncomfortable, or maybe you are one of my parents, siblings, other relatives, coworkers, neighbors, male friends, or perhaps even female friends you might want to decide to move right to the next chapter.

Since writing this was my decision and not necessarily that of my wonderful husband, I will keep mention of him to a minimum. It is important to note, however, that he is in fact wonderful, and I shared with him most of the struggles included. You will be able to figure out which ones were solely mine. In fact, they will be the parts that contain the TMI, so there you go.

I have a bit of a medical past that includes a pulmonary embolism at age 32 resulting in a lifelong prescription for blood thinners that enabled me to be part of a Coumadin club at my doctor's office with some lovely geriatric patients. When I had the embolism, I was clearly told by the hospital doctor that I should NEVER become pregnant. She said it just like that, with capital letters. At the time, I was just so thankful that I had survived the ordeal that I hadn't really considered the true effect her emphatic words would one day have on me.

Fast forward a few years, I had met and married the wonderful man mentioned earlier. Soon it was time to address the haunting words of that evil woman at the hospital. I mean the doctor, the nice doctor for whom I am so grateful. (Better?) I went to see various doctors and finally found my favorite person in the universe at a high risk pregnancy office. He looked over every paper provided and looked up at my desperate, frightened face and said,

"With close monitoring, there is no reason to think that you couldn't have a baby." He was lucky I didn't jump onto his lap and hug him to death. I was so relieved and happy, yet nervous and excited – all the things women feel when they decide starting a family is the right thing for them.

The first change I had to make was to switch from my regular blood thinner to a daily injection of Lovenox in my stomach. No more Coumadin club for a while. Millions of people do this every day. I pray for those people. I felt I could handle it for the next few months to maybe a little over a year. How was I to know that I would bruise like no one's business? Every day I added a great big palm sized black and blue to my stomach that contained a golf ball sized hard lump right in the center, painful to the touch. What a wonderful way to begin this exciting journey.

So much for my "few months to maybe a little over a year" theory. For the next many, very frustrating, months, we failed at conceiving. After a blood work up and visit with my OBGYN, I was given the first of many prescriptions that were going to help us along. However, that prescription was not my friend. I did not experience the terrible side effects many women do, so for that I was grateful, but it did nothing for me. Many more months went by. I know time supposedly flies, but when you are hoping and praying every single month that the little pink line will appear and it never does, it is like your world has stopped spinning. Millions of people experience such heartache daily. I pray for them. I knew I wasn't alone, but it was still awful. I based every decision I made during this time period on the thought that maybe I'd be pregnant. I even went as far as planning how we'd tell everyone. One April I was going to write our big news on Easter eggs.

Finally, I was sent to an office of reproductive specialists. I was part of a new, sadder group in a waiting room, longing for the days with my geriatric friends in the Coumadin club. Still, there were women there in worse situations than mine. There were cancer patients freezing eggs in hopes that they would not only survive their illnesses but also be able to have babies somehow someday. I pray for my waiting room group.

My new doctors took me off the prescribed medication since it hadn't helped. Serious monitoring had begun. These people needed to know the state of my reproductive system on a daily basis. I have never kept track so closely of anything before in my life. Needless to say, I had never reported such findings to anyone either. It is really a science and every aspect has to be addressed; the first day of the cycle, how many, if any, eggs are developing, the sizes of these eggs, which side they were on, the days of ovulation…it goes on and on. At some point you just have to listen to the parts that you can handle and trust that they are taking care of the rest because it's all too much. At first it is somewhat exciting, but after so many months of the same routine, it gets old, and more depressing.

At the start of my new regimen of alerting the media about my cycle, I was instructed to now add an ovulation test kit to my monthly activities. Just in case you are thinking to yourself, wow, she must have spent a fortune on sticks to urinate on, you are correct. Pregnancy tests were costly enough over the length of time I was purchasing them, but ovulation kits were ridiculous. I had strict instructions to call and make appointments the first time the ovulation test was positive. Sadly, that never happened and we were missing precious chances. Blood work, however, showed I was ovulating, yippee, the test sticks simply weren't responding to my urine. Who'd have thought that was possible? So, just to make things more interesting, I now had to go to the office to have blood drawn daily for weeks at a time. More days a month than not, I had to make the 45 minute drive in rush hour traffic to have blood drawn. In one 7 week period, I visited that office 35 times. Some days it wasn't just for blood work though. It gets more exciting than that. There were many days that my appointments included an internal sonogram too. Nothing like starting off the day like that!

The office scheduled these types of appointments from 6-9am. Most of the time, my wonderful husband came with me, which meant taking advantage of the earlier appointments so I could get him to the train station nearby in enough time for him to get to work. I didn't have to be at work until after 9am, so I spent many lonely mornings killing time. I used to buy one of those plastic bowls of cereal and a cup of milk at the little café in the building and sit in my car in the garage, sadly eating my Cheerios by myself. Sometimes I had Raisin Bran Crunch. There was a small park near my job where I could go for a little walk and just think before I went to work. Sometimes thinking was a good thing, other times, however, it was not. Mostly, I just prayed for help; for me and my sad group of waiting room friends.

At one point, somewhat early on, I was told I'd have the added pleasure of enduring a hysterosalpingogram. The dreaded HSG, possibly the lowest of my collective lows. The HSG is a type of dye contrast X-ray that checks to see if the fallopian tubes are open and the shape of the uterine cavity is normal. Another little piece of background information is that I have a dye contrast allergy. Knowing I cannot be given the contrast that they usually use, my doctor told me to let them know when I made the appointment for the procedure that I would need a different type of dye called Gadolinium. Let's just call it G for now. Being the good little direction follower I am, I made sure to mention the situation when I made the appointment on the exact day I was to call. The girl on the phone assured me they would be prepared for my special needs. Of course the test had to be on a very specific day during the cycle and I had to be pre-medicated for it. D was prescribed and instructions for some B and T were given. I met with the same doctor two more times before the procedure and both times, she questioned my inquiry about the radiology place having the G available. I reassured her that I did in fact ask, and the girl on the phone did in fact tell me they'd have it. I thought it was odd that she kept asking though, so I called and checked again. Thankfully, it was confirmed; all would be fine.

Procedure day arrived and I was terrified. My wonderful husband took time off to bring me. People were there for all different reasons, like any typical radiology office. I acted as if I was there for a routine thing, trying to convince myself I could handle this. Emotions were running strong and my nerves were getting the best of me as we waited. Then my name was called by someone who looked like she was going to be really nice and maybe hold my hand through this nightmare. She brought me to a small closet space where, after a hundred questions, I would change for the procedure. Only, while answering questions about my allergies, I reminded her about needing the G and she wasn't quite as reassuring as the faceless person on the phone. In fact, she told me special arrangements needed to be made for that and they weren't prepared; they had no G! Assuming she merely wasn't aware that I HAD made these arrangements. I calmly explained that I did check this out multiple times, that this was a time sensitive test, I needed to have it done that day, and that I had pre-medicated for it. Okay, I didn't calmly explain anything…I cried hysterically, bawled my eyes out, choking on my own saliva with mascara and snot dripping down my face. I trembled and cried harder than I had in any of the preceding months.

This was apparently my breaking point. She didn't know what to do with me. The best she could come up with was getting me a tissue and bringing me to a larger closet for multiple patients. She wanted to help me, I could tell, but there was literally nothing anyone could do, aside from finding a bottle of G and telling me we could proceed as planned. She briefly escaped the scene as I sat in my new, larger closet and sobbed with my face in my hands. Suddenly I felt a hand on my shoulder and heard a soothing voice with an accent from da islands, asking me why I was so upset. I sobbed through my words explaining the office error as best I could without giving away that I was a failure at conceiving. His calming voice and accent brought me to somewhat of a better place. I listened to his words that I don't recall, but I do know that whatever he said made sense and made me stop crying. As I struggled to use the tiny shredded remains of the one tissue I had been granted, I finally felt comfortable enough to pick up my head and open my swollen eyes to meet this soothing stranger.

There he was in his fancy gown, opening to the back of course, waiting for his knee x-ray. I mustered a smile and a thank you. Just then the seemingly nice woman came back, brought me into the narrow hallway and told me how sorry they all were and that they would explain to the reception idiot, I mean person, that she should have done things differently. Essentially, there was nothing that could be done that day and I would now lose another whole month. I wanted to run to the waiting room, find my wonderful husband and cry for the rest of the day, but first I had to say good bye to my new friend. I turned back to our closet, but he wasn't there. He had somehow vanished. I pray in gratitude for my guardian angel.

Sometimes I laugh when I think of that poor woman getting up that morning, heading out to work, probably stopping for some sort of coffee drink on the way, thinking she'd spend the day calling patients' names and leading them to a closet to tell them how to dress appropriately for whatever procedure they were having. Then, bam! She never saw it coming.

The test was rescheduled for the exact day it was to be performed. I am fairly certain everyone at that radiology office was well aware of the need to be prepared with some good, fresh G the day I came back. This time my very good friend brought me and I was confident things would go more smoothly. I was pre-medicated again and ready to get this show on the road. I revisited my small closet to change, walked into the x-ray room, and hopped up onto a hard, flat, cold table. It was time to meet the man who would perform the procedure. Women go through painstaking efforts to find the gynecologist they are the least uncomfortable with, yet here I was with this complete stranger eager to begin. During the test, the G is injected through a device called a cannula into the uterus and tubes. It felt like gallons of G were going in. The procedure was as awkward and uncomfortable as you can imagine, but it was not painful and I was grateful for that.

When it was finally done, the doctor left the room and the woman, who had stayed for the show, gave me instructions. I was to get down from the table using a small step stool and walk to the bathroom to change. Hmmm, so you just filled me with fluid and now I have to stand up? I felt foolish asking but I had to know – wasn't this going to come pouring out of me? She reminded me that she had already stated there was the paper "modesty" sheet covering me that I could use for any leaking fluid and there were pads in the bathroom I was welcome to use, as if they were my parting gift. Was she serious? I actually envisioned blue liquid (I'm not sure why G is blue in my imagination) cascading out of my body as I tried to waddle across the room to the bathroom holding a paper sheet in place to absorb any leaking G. I was stunned by my instructions, but again, followed with precision. It really wasn't as bad as I thought. I am not sure where all the G went but it wasn't the waterfall I anticipated. I was done, it was over and I didn't even cry that day at all. The results showed everything was fine and normal. I went home and napped.

Every now and then at this office of reproductive specialists, we'd meet with a doctor and discuss the next steps. After a great deal of monitoring, seemingly gallons of blood drawn, too many internal sonos to count, and the horrific HSG experiences (plural), they decided to take another approach. It was time for intrauterine insemination, IUI. The blood draws and sonos continued and the IUIs were performed at the exact right times on the exact days on which they needed to be performed to be successful, supposedly.

The first IUI attempt failed. Another month later, the second IUI attempt failed. Another month later, the third IUI attempt failed. See where I am going? Month after month, we went through the emotional ups and downs, the excitement that maybe this was it, the let down of learning no it wasn't, and the physical discomfort of the needles, internal sonos, and procedures only to find out the attempts all failed. My wonderful husband accompanied me for all but one attempt. He could not miss work that day. Of course, that was the one time the procedure hurt more than anything and I ended up bawling my eyes out again. There was one nice nurse type of person in the room who seemed to care and she gave me some water and a tissue (again, just the one tissue, I don't know why these places can't toss a girl the box!) and allowed me to remain in the dark room for a little bit before making me hop up and leave, freeing the room for the next patient on the assembly line.

Because they were taking a more cautious approach with me, we hung onto the hope that an IUI would work and continued trying more times than most patients. After the seventh failed attempt, I felt defeated. Seven more lost months later, we were still failing at conceiving. I prayed harder.

When it was clear that the IUIs weren't going to work, the discussions turned to IVF. There were many concerns to consider. My medical past and the need to take hormones that would increase the risk of having another blood clot was the main concern. In fact, one of the many informational sheets we received had four warnings about the risks of blood clotting. Of course, for us, the financial impact was another big concern. The cost of all the test kits was nothing compared to the copays every single time I went to the office, whether I was there for a two minute blood test, an internal sono, a procedure, or a meeting with a doctor. Still, all of that didn't compare to this next step; it was going to be a huge expense. I am forever grateful to the insurance company we had at the time for covering so much, but when contracts as detailed as those used for mortgages were presented to be signed, we knew this was serious.

Decision making time was a good few weeks. We had to attend IVF orientations and injection classes where light refreshments were served. There was a tour of the IVF center and the OR across the hall. There were quite a few meetings with the doctors who had to okay this venture. I needed letters from the hematologist stating I could go ahead with this plan, and I had to write one stating that I was aware of the risk I was taking by entering into this process.

Turns out these timely protocols were a blessing. I needed time to think. I wasn't sure if this was the right thing for us, for me. We had invested so much time into fulfilling this dream of ours, but I wasn't sure risking my own life was the right choice. Other people seemed quite willing to risk my own life for it and that kind of bothered me, to tell you the truth. Then there was the financial consideration. The insurance company had given us a total available amount that we could use toward this goal and we had been chipping away at that sum for more than just one calendar of time. We wondered if perhaps an adoption was a more sensible direction since IVF had no guarantees and we could only undergo the process once before depleting the available funds. So I just prayed more and more, with my prayers becoming dramatically more desperate. In fact, I often prayed until tears streamed down my face. I just needed to know if this was the right decision.

I used to walk for two hours a day and, while enjoying my Blast from the Past play list, I prayed for signs that would lead me in the right direction. I needed to know if we should proceed with caution or abandon ship and take a different approach to having a family. I am a firm believer in spiritual presence, always have been. For example, I know the two swans in the yard on my wedding day were my grandparents who had just passed letting me know they were there with me. As I walked, I noted my exact thoughts each time I saw a cardinal. One day, two playfully flew just ahead of me for a whole block. Little by little I was becoming convinced all signs were leading toward moving forward with the plans. I believe all the emails I received right when I needed them most were signs. You know the one that starts with "God has seen you struggling... God says it's over." I still have that one saved in my New Mail since 2008! I received one once that had a picture of a cat dangling from a bar and it said something to the effect of "faith means letting go." I am not a big cat person, but that one spoke to me. I realized I just had to let go and have faith that this was the right thing and God would take care of me. Suddenly, I felt empowered, relieved, and thrilled by the thought of undergoing the next phase of achieving our dream! I had total faith this was how we would come to meet the baby that was meant to be ours. I knew it and I was ready, anxious and eager to get things started.

With pens in hand, we met once again with a team from the office and started signing our lives away, with no trepidation. We had to make decisions about what we would do if multiple eggs fertilized. Would we try transferring all or store them? What would we do with them if one of us became incapacitated in some way? What if I became too old or otherwise unable to carry others later on? Would we discard or donate them? Would someone else carry them for us? What if we ended up no longer married, what if one or both of us died? All really pleasant thoughts as we embarked on this exciting adventure. There was also the financial piece; signing that we were made fully aware of the expenses: the parts of the surgical procedures that were not going to be covered, the annual storage fees…my hand hurt by the end of the meeting.

Naturally, there was a great deal of monitoring, tracking, and reporting to accomplish. They stressed that precise timing is required. There was also a whole lot of organization involved. The drugs had to be given at certain times and most pharmacies don't have them readily available, so they had to be ordered and delivered from far away. Before finding a pharmacy on our plan only an hour away that carried everything, the drugs were flying across nine states for the next day's use! I was so filled with faith that it would all be fine that I didn't even worry about my drugs having a lay over and missing their connecting flight, unable to reach me. It was so freeing to be able to step back and trust that things were exactly as they were meant to be.

There were DVD tutorials for injections that had to be given in various body parts. We had leaflets and diagrams in addition to the notes we had taken in class. Drug arrival night was a strange experience. A man came to the door with a huge bag. It seemed so suspicious at the time. This delivery guy drove over an hour to get this package to me. I always wondered if he was at all curious about its contents. Pardon the spellings, but that great big bag contained boxes of some Ganarelix, Novarel, Endometrin, a little Bravelle, and a pinch of Menapur, among others. There were pens with pre-measured doses and syringes with tiny little vials. We had learned how to measure and combine exactly how much I was instructed to use of each at very specific times. Some needles were long and some short. We, my wonderful husband and I, were nervous but excited to start and I had total faith it was going to go smoothly.

Now, before you go feeling sorry for this pin cushion, I should let you know that I did get two days off from my daily Lovenox shots. The day before and the day of the egg retrieval surgery, I was not allowed to take the blood thinner, which of course had to be cleared by other doctors. Waiting for the call to find out which day and what time the retrieval would be was intense. Not knowing made planning things difficult. I didn't know what, if any, days we'd have to take off work, if I'd have to concoct some reasons to be unable to take part in weekend activities, or when I would have to prepare for the surgery the same way one prepares for a colonoscopy, as if everything else going on wasn't quite enough. Finally, the call came. Day 16 of the cycle was going to be the big day!

As we drove around and around the parking garage climbing to our usual level, we suddenly realized something - we were going across the hall! It was the first time we walked out of the elevator and made a left. It felt so right, not a doubt in my mind about anything. We arrived in the OR suite at our assigned time and I was given instructions about my outfit for the procedure. I changed into my seemingly unnecessary gown, gave myself a lovely updo to be contained within an equally as lovely cap, and slipped into my non-slip slippers. I had a bed, my wonderful husband by my side, and complete faith in God. I watched how busy everyone was. I saw patients wheeled in and out, some for the first time like myself, and others for their second and third rounds of IVF. I prayed for all of us.

They wheeled me to the OR, I got a kiss goodbye, and in I went. I paid close attention to each person and had a clear understanding of what the anesthesiologist told me to expect. At least, I thought I did. She explained that I'd first feel drunk, then dizzy. Only, I felt those in the opposite order. I tried to inquire if that was okay. I think I got as far as "wait, is it o…" I woke up back where I had started and the next patient was already being wheeled in. Recovery was not long and I was homeward bound.

It was time to wait for the next call that would tell us when to come in for the second procedure when the fertilized eggs would be transferred back in. That call came on day 18. It seemed like all good news; five eggs were retrieved, four were mature (which made me giggle picturing one immature egg sticking its tongue out at the others in a nanny nanny poo poo kind of way) and could be used, and three had fertilized and would be transferred during the procedure to take place on day 19 precisely at 10am. This was so exciting! While keeping in mind that we could still find out the process didn't work, it was impossible to not think about the reality that we could have triplets! We never dreamed of having three babies, here we were all along just hoping for one. This was unbelievable and we were thrilled by the news and excited to go back that Saturday for my 10am transfer procedure.

Unlike the surgical retrieval, I would be awake for this. My instructions were pretty simple; drink at least 16 ounces of water an hour before the procedure so the bladder is full at the appointment time. The fuller the better. My thought process was as follows; if fuller was better, I should maybe drink even more than just the 16 ounces. I don't know how much I drank, but I had never been so physically uncomfortable. It didn't matter though; this was the most important day of our lives.

I was so grateful for my newfound faith that things were perfect because there were a few minor snafus. First, I was genuinely afraid I'd lose bladder control mid procedure, perhaps all over the doctor. Then, I learned the doctor who was performing all the procedures that morning was the one who hurt me during that one IUI when I was alone. I hadn't seen him since and had hoped to never see him again. It was disappointing, but I was still okay with it. The worst was that after stressing the importance of the meticulous timing every single step of the way, my procedure was pushed back for about an hour and a half without explanation. They just kept saying the doctor would be there as soon as possible. I don't think they understood the intensity of the bladder issue. I prayed for my fellow full bladder sufferers as we all patiently waited.

The doctor finally came in and was quite apologetic for the lengthy wait. He explained that they would be transferring three fertilized eggs; 7A, 7A, and 7B. I thought maybe I was supposed to know what that meant so I didn't say anything. After all, it didn't really matter, I was just praying I didn't urinate in his face. Apparently, those were the sizes and grades with A being the best grade an egg could get. Honestly, it still meant nothing to me. I told him my concerns about his safety during the procedure and he assured me no patient had ever lost control of her bladder on the table. I was oddly honored to possibly be the first.

After watching two other women being wheeled in and out of the OR, it was finally my turn, not a second too soon.

This time, my wonderful husband was able to join me in the OR and we were able to watch on the screen as the three fertilized eggs were placed. I love that I was able to watch the process; it was an added bonus I wasn't expecting. I cried as I was wheeled back to recovery, mainly because I had to go to the bathroom so badly and was afraid they'd somehow fall out if I went right away, but also because one of the women in the OR wished me a happy Mother's Day a day early. Of course there was no way of knowing the outcome, but I knew in my heart it was going to secretly be a happy Mother's Day for me.

It was suggested to not use a pregnancy test stick at home before finding out from blood work, but I couldn't resist. One night, I just took out another stick and held my breath waiting for the lines to appear. I couldn't believe my eyes, not only did it respond to my urine, but it was positive! Hip hip hooray for us! I showed my wonderful husband and we had a cautiously celebratory moment. My appointment for blood work was the next day. The call we received after that was saved on our answering machine for a long time, "Nora, you are pregnant!" It was the first time someone from that office sounded happy on the phone and I appreciated her excitement for us.

The first sono was performed and the girl nonchalantly said, "You have two." I am so grateful for those two that you can't imagine, but I guess after thinking for those few weeks that there would be three, I was a little saddened by her discovery. Where was my third? She explained that it simply didn't implant and just sort of disappeared. She added that a third would have made my pregnancy more difficult and they likely would have been born too early, posing risks to their health and my own. It was sad, but I had faith this was exactly how it was supposed to be. I was having twins and we were over the moon with excitement, gratitude, happiness, and relief. We were given some time in the room for an actual celebratory moment before leaving. I was careful to not have my sonogram pictures in my hands as I left, remembering how it felt to see others' pictures when I was still part of the sad waiting room group. To this day, I still think about my number three and wonder.

My past struggles have given me so many people to include in my prayers. I pray for all the women who long to have a baby. I pray for my waiting room friends in both offices. I pray for my angel that his knee is okay and he is doing well, if he really existed. I pray for anyone who gives themselves shots because I disposed of well over one thousand needles and - ouch! I pray for moms of multiples, because I am right there with you girlfriends! Finally, I pray for my number three who possibly saved the lives or preserved the health of his or her siblings and mother.

My new beautiful is not being a mother. That's not to say that being a mom isn't a beautiful thing, it surely is, but to me, my new beautiful is the strengthened faith I gained while handling my struggles. I was cool as a cucumber throughout my pregnancy, despite the five high risk categories I had the privilege to fall into. There was simply a newer, stronger part of me that accepted there was a reason for everything and it was all part of God's plan. It might seem easy for me to say because I have my perfect twins. They are my dreams come true, but my faith extends beyond them. We might never come to realize why we are led down certain paths in life, but knowing it is meant to be is somewhat freeing. Please don't misunderstand me, a lot of things still hurt badly, but it is a little easier to come to terms with the pain when you can see it as part of a plan that is merely still unknown to us.

Stronger faith is my *New Beautiful*.

Mom's Strength

Mom would always say "We make plans and God laughs." Well ain't that the truth!

My mom was diagnosed with Stage 4 breast cancer and told she had 3 months to live. Talk about a change of plans! There were two ways she could have gone: either say goodbye to all of her loved ones and wait it out OR fight like hell. Well, she was a fighter and fought for nine <u>years!</u>

Mom taught us life is about choices. You can choose to give up or choose to fight. You can choose to be negative or choose to be positive. You can choose to be sad or choose to be happy. She decided to always fight, be positive, be happy. She would say "Someone always has it worse than me."

I was twenty-four years old when my mom was diagnosed, a baby. As a girl you never really picture what life without your mom would be like, but at thirty-three that is my reality. I am engaged to an amazing man. Who pictures a bride without her mother by her side? Who pictures starting a family without calling your mom? This is a new life. My life without calling my mom every day. A life without my mom. Well to be honest… IT SUCKS! But I have a choice as she taught us. I can stop living my life and be sad all the time. I could sit and feel sorry for myself, or I can live my life the way she did…always choosing the positive. Well I can't let her down. I choose to live my life. Will I cry? Sure. But I will think of her strength. Did she cry? …No.

Mom spent nine years trying treatment, after treatment. If one stopped working, she would just ask "What is the next trial drug you can put me on?" She did this all with such grace and dignity. At times you even forgot she was sick. She would tell us that the disease was worse for us than her. She put others first. I knew my mom was an amazing woman but she was my mom and I was a little bias. I knew she inspired me to never give up, to live your best life, but again she was my mom.

At my mom's funeral every seat in the church was filled. Not only did people come to say goodbye, but also to show their appreciation for someone who touched their lives. I want her legacy to be that person who teaches others to choose to be happy, to choose to live their best life. Life is not what we plan. Our family didn't plan to lose our mom so soon but those were the cards we were dealt. We have to choose now how to live our life without her.

Every day I will choose to be happy. On my wedding day, I will choose to see that it is the day I start my new family with my amazing husband. I will not focus how much I will miss my mom because that is not what she taught me. With her always in my heart, I have chosen to start a *New Beautiful* life.

FULL CIRCLE

I was born, June 5, 1932. I have two sisters. I was the "baby sister." I have enjoyed the most wonderful life. My mom, Josephine, and my Dad, Samuel, were terrific parents who made sure we always had good times. We lived on the water and enjoyed years of sailing and boating. I learned to swim well at age two. I fell into a canal that was full of horseshoe crabs. I was afraid of them and I didn't want my feet to touch the bottom, so I just started swimming to get away. Life seemed so easy then.

I went to elementary school, and then on to high school. I had a very good singing voice and sang in many shows in elementary and high school. We all loved our music Director, Mr. B. I was also a majorette. I belonged to the Lucie Society. You had to be very popular before they would invite you to join. I was very lucky to have so many good friends. We used to be called the sexy six. We couldn't have been less sexy though.

I met my husband in 1950 when he was in the US Air Force stationed locally to where I lived. At the time we met, I was actually engaged to another man who happened to be very wealthy. But when I met this man dressed in his Air Force uniform, standing on the side of the road hitch hiking, I couldn't believe my eyes. I had to pick him up. It was truly love at first sight. I broke off the engagement and I was married to the love of my life one year later and honeymooned in West Virginia.

My husband was a very good Catholic and wouldn't use birth control. My first son was born 9 months later. After that, we did use birth control. After my husband got out of the service, we moved back to the beach community where I grew up. We lived with my parents and saved money for a home of our own.

We did save money and were able to buy our *dream* home. Our second son was born. It was the time of the baby boom and on our block alone, there were 106 children. Some homes at eight kids alone. What fun the children had each day. The women were all friendly. It was a lovely place to live. The children never left the block because they had it all. Swimming lessons in the canal, fun on our boat, and they played all day and night.

But there was one nightmare I will never forget. One of the most traumatic times in my life. The baker would walk house to house to sell whatever was in his basket for the day. So he would leave his truck in the middle of the street, fill his basket and walk house to house. When he came to the door, you could buy bread, or buns or cakes. As he was selling, my younger son jumped in his truck to play around and pretend he was driving. When the baker ran toward to truck yelling at him, my son jumped out into the middle of the street and as he jumped a car hit him. Almost three weeks of being hospitalized, part of the time he was in a coma. My heart has never ached so much. I shed many tears and worries. Luckily, at age eight he was quite a fighter and survived.

We lived in that house for twenty six years and built a family and life there. Life was good. Then it was time to close that chapter and move into a life of retirement. We moved into a condo in Florida. We moved from one friendly community to another. We enjoyed it so much. You can't beat the Florida weather year round. We lived there for another twenty six years. We lived across the street from the beach and had a community pool. We dined with friends almost nightly. Our daily events included shows, plays, musicals, shopping, and picnics. We celebrated birthdays, anniversaries, and any happy occasion we could think of. For many years, we were snowbirds too. So we would fly or drive back north for summers with our family.

Years later, everyone started moving out of the condo complex, so it was our turn. We sold the condo and bought a house in a community not too far away. What a big mistake. We missed family and missed friends. Living in a house is a lot more isolating than a condo. We were getting older and did not go out as much. We decided to sell and move back north. Although we wanted to move, we also were at a time in our life that we needed to be around family. We took a big loss when we sold the Florida house. But we had a lot to gain moving back "home." After all these years, my husband (age 85) and myself (age 83) have come full circle, right back where we started a life together.

My husband and I have enjoyed a wonderful life. We worked very hard over the years but that's not what gave us so much. It was friends and family. Our great grandchildren are a complete joy. We are just so proud of our family. May God give us a few more years. My three granddaughters have given us so much joy and happiness that we will never forget. We have shared so many good times, good vacations and they continue to go on. My sons have been the most wonderful sons, so loving, so caring. Oh how much fun we had raising them, so many wonderful memories. My daughter in-laws have shown so much care and love to us. We have all had so many great laughs.

One son said to me, "Mom will you ever grow up?" and my answer to him was "I hope not." Life is fantastic, enjoy every day to the fullest. I wish I could thank each person who has made my life happy. I would thank them with all my heart for everything they have shared with us and for showing so much love. Family is what life is all about, and we have the best.

As I reflect on the theme of this book with my granddaughter, it may appear that I have not written enough about the challenges that I have faced and overcome. But with years experience, I think the message that has made me a *New Beautiful*, is that life is meant to be enjoyed, despite all the challenges that we are presented. When I think of my *New Beautiful*, it is redefining beauty along the path of your life. These wrinkles and wig tell a beautiful story you know… one of true love. I could have written about one of my most traumatic happenings: when I was diagnosed with breast cancer about ten years ago: a mastectomy, radiation, medications, and doctor appointments- it was all traumatizing. I also broke a hip: pain, agony, surgery, physical therapy. I witnessed my parents passing away and many of my friends as well. We lived through poor times, really poor times. We lived through times of war. We lived through many historical depressing events. But when I reflect on my life, those weren't my defining moments or memories, the happy ones were. I do believe though that it was those challenges that, collectively, made me the woman I am today.

When I moved back north and realized my life had been lived full circle, I realized I traveled the world, moved across states and did the things I wanted to in order to be happy. I feel like it was all supposed to happen this way now that I have returned "home." I live like every day is Christmas… it's a gift and for this I believe I'm constantly redefining a *New Beautiful*.

Printed in the United States
By Bookmasters